WHAT
IS
KOREAN
BUDDHISM?

This is the book for anyone who is curious about Korean Buddhism. It offers a wide range of information, from history to temple life to monk's to tours of the more famous temples, leaving the deeper, more philosophical side to a later date. Some of the articles included here are for the beginner and some for the more scholarly searcher. At the back there are a few of the main chants and some teachings for inspiration.

Ven.Jeong Dae
President
Korean Buddhist Chogye Order

FOREWORD

This is the book for anyone who is curious about Korean Buddhism. It offers a wide range of information, from history to temple life to monk's to tours of the more famous temples, leaving the deeper, more philosophical side to a later date. Some of the articles included here are for the beginner and some for the more scholarly searcher. At the back there are a few of the main chants and some teachings for inspiration.

Korean Buddhism is a living tradition which is difficult to become familiar with because of the lack of available material in languages other than Korean and Chinese characters. The Hermit Kingdom, as Korea was sometimes called, has not been any more open in the Buddhist field than in any other. Therefore many aspects of Korean Buddhism remain beyond the reach of interested people and this is only recently beginning to change. In the last few years, a number of new books have come out but there is still nothing which offers a basic introduction. Therefore we decided to put together this material. It is mostly taken from articles that we have written; there are three excellent articles written by others also included, adapted to the present volume.

We have tried hard to make the material correct, interesting and useful. To these ends, we have opted for a rather unusual style. Interjected into the text at the appropriate points are articles which enlarge upon a particular aspect. As the style of this information is different, the reader may find the jolt strange. Therefore we have begun and ended each article with a lotus flower so that the item can be skipped and read later if the reader so wishes.

The book opens with a look at the history from two perspectives. This leads into a consideration of the features which make Korean Buddhism individual. Monastic life follows with details on the ordination and activities of monks. Here we have included two long articles on bhikkunis because there is much interst in ordained women today and they are so little known. The first concerns the history which is often speculative because of the lack of records. The second is a modern article about how ordained women live. The next section, Visiting Temples, is all about how to go to a temple and what you will see. After that we have written about the main temples of Korea incorporating information about different subjects into the narrative. Thus dragons are dealt with in the article on Yongju-sa, for example. As many visitors have no time to travel away from Seoul, we decided to give an overview of some of the principle temples of the capital. The book terminates with a few chants and teachings of Korean monks. At the back, in the Appendix, there is a short glossary of some of the more special terms used in the book as well as a list of the kings with their dates. There is no index because we felt that the material lent itself well to a detailed contents instead.

We hope that many people will be spurred on to read more about Korean Buddhism, visit the temples and thus become familiar with a rich tradition which offers the teachings of the Buddha in different, simpler trappings than those we are more familiar with.

May all beings be well and happy!

CONTENTS

Chapter I

THE HISTORY OF KOREAN BUDDHISM

THE HISTORY OF KOREAN BUDDHISM

I n order to understand Korean Buddhism, we must first take a look at its history. Although there is evidence of earlier contact with Buddhism, the usually accepted date for the introduction of Buddhism to the peninsula from China is 372 CE (Common Era). Today Buddhism is woven into every aspect of Korean culture from customs to artifacts.

Early Days

Shamanism

Although there is evidence of earlier contact with Buddhism, the usually accepted date for the introduction of Buddhism to the peninsula from China is 372 CE (Common Era).

When Buddhism was first brought from China to the Korean Peninsula in 372 CE, Shamanism was the indigenous religion. Shamanism is the ancient religion of animism and nature-spirit worship and its origins in Korea are lost in antiquity. It is based on the belief that human beings as well as natural forces and inanimate objects all possess spirits or that they are gods. Since Buddhism was not seen to be in conflict with the rites of nature worship, it was able to naturally blend in with Shamanism. And so many of the special mountains believed to be the residences of gods in pre-Buddhist times, soon became the sites of Buddhist temples.

Korean Shamanism regarded three gods with special reverence and importance: the Mountain God, Sanshin (who is usually depicted as an old man with a tiger at his feet), the Toksong, or recluse, and Ch'ilsong (the god of the seven stars, the Big Dipper). Buddhism accepted and

The Spirit of the Seven Stars

absorbed these three gods and, even today, special shrines are set aside for them in most temples. The Mountain God, in particular, receives due veneration following the ceremonies honoring the Buddha in the Main Hall.

And thus Chinese Buddhism blended with Korean Shamanism to produce a unique form: Korean Buddhism. As in other Buddhist countries, the fundamental teachings of the Buddha remained the same, even though the form, influenced by indigenous culture and customs, was uniquely Korean.

Information about the Karak Kingdom is of particular interest because the princess came from a Buddhist stronghold in India and most probably brought statues and texts with her.

The Recluse

Koguryo

In 372 CE, a monk was invited from China to the northern Kingdom of Koguryo. He brought Chinese texts and statues with him. Buddhism was quickly accepted by the Koguryo royalty and their subjects.

This original Buddhism was elementary in form. The people believed in the law of cause and effect – "as you sow, so shall you reap" – and the search after happiness. This simple philosophy had much in common with the indigenous Shaman beliefs and may have been a reason for the quick assimilation of Buddhism by the people of Koguryo.

Buddha Triad Carved on Rock Surface.
(In Sosan, Paekje. Nat'l Treasure No.84)

Paekje

Buddhism was carried from Koguryo to the southwestern kingdom of Paekje in 384 CE and there, too, the royal family received it first. The teaching seems to have been similar to that in Koguryo. King Asin (r. 392-405), for example, proclaimed that his " people should believe in Buddhism and seek happiness." In the reign of King Song (r. 523-554), there is a record of a monk, Kyomik, returning from India with new texts and especially the Vinaya (monks' rules and the stories leading to their formulation). He is considered the founder of one of the main schools of Buddhism of that period.

From 530 on, monks traveled to Japan and there taught the people Buddhism. Architects, painters, potters and other craftsman and artists often accompanied the monks and it was these people who constructed the great temples of Japan.

Karak

For a short time, a small, separate federation known as the Karak Kingdom (1st to 6th century CE) existed. It was a small kingdom in the Kimhae area situated on the southern coast between mighty Paekje and fast-growing Shilla. Kaya could not repel an invasion in the mid-sixth century and so was annexed to Shilla before reaching full maturity.

The Samguk-yusa says that there was a stone pagoda in

THE THREE
KINGDOMS

5th Century

Koguryo

• P'yongyang

• Jungjin
(Kongju)   Shilla

• Sabi   Kumsong
(Puyo)   (Kyongju) •

Paekje

Karak

Cheju Island

Hogye-sa in Kimhae. This pagoda had four sides and
five storeys, and the carvings on the sides
were famous for their magnificence. It is
known that this pagoda was brought by
sea to Korea by an Indian princess
from Ayudhya a kingdom of
southern India. She came to marry
King Suro (r. 42-199) the first king
of Karak and she was later known
as Queen Hohwang-ok. As far as
the records show, until the arrival of
the Indian princess, there were no temples
and no Buddha statues and the people
knew nothing about Buddhism. Because of
this, there was no place to keep the pagoda.
It was only later, in 452, in the 2nd year of the
8th Karak king, Chilji (r. 451-492), that Wanghu-sa
was built.

Information about the Karak Kingdom is of particular
interest because the princess came from a Buddhist
stronghold in India and most probably brought
statues and texts with her. However, according to
the above record, Buddhism was not popular in
Karak before the building of the temple. This is
not surprising considering that this would
mean that Buddhism was accepted in Karak
before Shilla and even before Koguryo.
Unfortunately, we know very little about
Karak but there are a few legends
concerning Buddhism told about the
kingdom.

One is about the story of King Suro's
decision on where to place the capital of Karak.
Another is about Mano-sa (the temple of 10,000
fish). There are also two stories one about the
temple Changyu-sa and another about the
hermitage Ch'ilbul-am. But these stories do not necessarily
contain any historical truth and so cannot be considered too
seriously. Till we have certain new historical evidence, we
must think of the above legends as indications of Karak
Buddhism only.

Shilla

In Shilla, it was the common people who were first attracted to Buddhism. Among some of the aristocrats, there was considerable resistance to the new culture. It was only after the martyrdom of Ich'adon, in the reign of King Pophung (r. 514-540) in 527 CE, that Buddhism gradually became the national religion of Shilla.

There we read that Master Ado stayed at Morye's house for a number of years with his three attendants and then he returned healthy to Koguryo.

Stories about the arrival of Buddhism in Shilla

Firstly, "the Koguryo monk, Ado, came to Shilla in the 2nd year (263) of the reign of the 13th King Mich'u (r. 262-284)." This information comes from a record quoted in Samguk-yusa. Master Ado's father was an envoy to Koguryo and his mother, a Koguryo woman, was called Kodonyong. Ado went to Wei to meet his father at the age of 16 and then he studied under Master Hsuan-chang. He returned to Koguryo when he was 19 and went to Shilla to teach Buddhism, following his mother's advice. This was in 263, the 2nd year of King Mich'u. Before journeying to Shilla, Master Ado heard from his mother that there were seven temple sites in Shilla where the past seven Buddhas had been. But when he tried to teach Buddhism to the Shilla people, they tried to kill him. Ado hid himself at the house of Morye at Ilsson and stayed there until he cured a daughter of King Mich'u of a terrible sickness. Only then, was he able to build a temple in Ch'on-gyong forest and teach Buddhism. As soon as King Mich'u died, the people tried once more to harm him. And so he returned to Morye's house and lived there till he died.

Secondly, we have another record concerning a different monk. "Master Mukhoja stayed at the house of Morye at Ilsson in the reign of the 19th King Nulji (r. 417-458)." This is quoted in the Samguk-yusa. Mukhoja secretly lived in the cellar inside Morye's house and then left. Before he left, he taught the people about the use of incense, and he cured another princess.

Thirdly, we have another reference to Master Ado. "Master Ado came to Morye's house with

Stone Buddha(Bori-sa temple site, Shilla, Treasure No. 136)

Seated Buddha Traid(Shilla)

three attendants and stayed there, in the reign of King Pich'o (r. 479-500)." There we read that Master Ado stayed at Morye's house for a number of years with his three attendants and then he returned healthy to Koguryo. He left his three attendants in Shilla to teach sutras and the Vinaya and they made many followers. This record adds that Ado looked like Master Mukhoja.

Fourthly, Master Ado came to Morye's house on the 11th of the 3rd month, 527, the 14th year of King Pophung. Morye, on seeing Ado, was surprised and frightened. He hid Master Ado in a secret place inside his house, explaining that two Koguryo monks, Chongbang and Myolguch'e who had come before him had been killed. And so Morye cared for and served Master Ado. Just at that time, Ado found out that a foreign envoy had brought incense to King Pophung. And so Master Ado went to the palace. The foreign envoy showed Master Ado respect and "this showed the king, for the first time, that Buddhist monks should be respected. The king then allowed Buddhism to be accepted."

This record is of particular value as it introduces a new aspect of the beginning of Buddhism in the Shilla Kingdom. At first the two monks were martyred. Then the king accepted Buddhism after seeing the foreign envoy show respect to Master Ado. Here the martyrdom of Ich'adon is not mentioned, unlike other records.

According to the four above records, there are three different Master Ados who introduced Buddhism to Shilla. Though the contents are very similar, the chronology of events is unreliable. We must therefore conclude that we can neither know who introduced Buddhism to Shilla nor when it was introduced precisely. The above records are all legends which were handed down among the people and it seems that the transmission was not achieved on the level of a national exchange but rather as a continuous series of missions of monks. Legends tell us that a few Koguryo monks secretly introduced Buddhism again and again, and that the area they worked in was around Ilsson and especially Morye's house. The missionary monks were not just one or two, they were many. Also they had to work secretly without revealing their proper names or identity.

In addition, the names, Mukhoja and Ado (or Adu), might not be the specific names of individual monks, but words used to indicate monks in general. For we are told that "... when the name of a monk is not known, he was called `Adu-samma.'" This is the long form of "Adu" or "Ado," a common name for a monk.

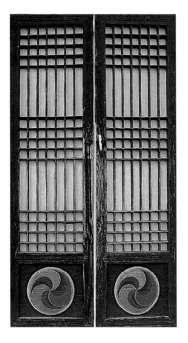

Since Buddhism was introduced to Shilla in that way, we can guess that the next king, Chinhung (r. 540-576), wanted to make Buddhism official as soon as he acceded to the throne.

Since Buddhism was introduced to Shilla in that way, we can guess that the next king, Chinhung (r. 540-576), wanted to make Buddhism official as soon as he acceded to the throne. However, this was not to be. Stubborn, conservative ministers and officials of the court objected to Buddhism. King Chinhung, who was deeply convinced that Buddhism would bring good fortune to the people and help his kingdom, was greatly troubled by the resistance of his ministers. It was under these circumstances that a young minister, Ich'adon, knowing the king's problems, died a martyr for the kingdom, the king, and Buddhism.

The Story of Ich'adon

In the Samguk-sagi and the Samguk-yusa, Ich'adon is said to have been a nephew of King Pophung. The Samguk-yusa adds that Ich'adon's grandfather, Ajinjong, was a son of Suppogalmun. According to the Samguk-sagi, Suppogalmun was the father of the 22nd king, Chijung (r. 500-514) whose son was King Pophung. Therefore King Pophung was Ich'adon's uncle.

According to the story, Ich'adon decided to help the king and so he and the king developed a plan which would finally convince the ministers. At that time, anyone who claimed they were a Buddhist was beheaded. And so, according to the plan, one day Ich'adon proclaimed his belief and the king ordered him to be beheaded. Ich'adon announced, "If Buddhism is good then, when my head is cut, the blood that flows will be white." True to his belief, as soon as his head was severed from his body, white blood poured out. Seeing the greatness of Ich'adon's sacrifice, the ministers no longer objected to Buddhism and it was accepted from then on.

One year later, in 528, King Pophung ordered that the people cease from killing any living things. In 535, King Pophung started to build Hungnyun-sa in Ch'on-gyong forest which was east of Kumkyo, the bridge over the river So-ch'on in Kyongju. When some parts of the temple had been completed, the king went to live in the temple and ordained as a monk; he took the Buddhist name of Popkong, meaning "Dharma Emptiness." The queen followed her husband's example and, when Yonghung-sa had been built, she was ordained and took the Buddhist name of Myobop, meaning "Marvelous Dharma."

Thus Buddhism was established in Shilla during the reign of King Pophung. Apart from the few legends mentioned, we know nothing of the policy and achievements of Buddhism in the reign of King Pophung.

Stele for the Martyred Ich'a-don.

The Patronage of Buddhism by King Chinhung

Shilla Buddhism did not take on its own specific character until the reign of King Chinhung (r. 540-576), the 24th king of the Shilla Kingdom. He, through his policies, was responsible for the unique nature of Shilla Buddhism and the immense impact which it had on the culture of Korea.

In 540, King Chinhung ascended the throne when he was still young and so his mother ruled Shilla as regent. King Chinhung was a devoted Buddhist throughout his life and his achievements as a Buddhist have been carefully recorded, here are some:

* In 544, Hungnyun-sa was completed and in the 3rd month of that year many men and women were ordained as bhikkus and bhikkunis.

* In spring 549, an envoy from Liang brought the Shilla monk, Master Kaktok, who had been studying in Liang, back with a Buddha relic. At that time the king told all his ministers to go and bow out of respect in front of the temple.

Three-storied stone Pagoda on Kamunsa temple site (Shilla, Nat'l Treasure No. 112)

* In 550, the king appointed Master Anjang to an important government post.

* In 551, the king nominated Master Hyeryang from Koguryo to be the leader of the monks and entrusted him with all sorts of plans to make Buddhism grow and prosper. Hyeryang held large Buddhist assemblies for the first time.

* In 565, an envoy, Liu-ssu from Ch'en, and Master Ming-kuan brought about 1,700 volumes of sutras and sastras to Shilla.

* In 566, the temples Hwangnyong-sa, (which had been commenced 13 years earlier), Kiwon-sa, and Shilje-sa were completed.

* On the 20th day of the 10th month, 572, a huge ceremony was held for the war dead at Oe-sa for seven days.

* In 574, the king made three Buddha statues at Hwangnyong-sa.

* In 576, Master Anhong came back from China and he offered the Lankavatara-sutra,

the Srimala-sutra, and Buddha relics to the king.

All of these records show that King Chinhung promoted Buddhism very enthusiastically. Not only did he believe in Buddhism fervently, building temples, ordaining bhikkus and bhikkunis, and doing other Buddhist work, but he also applied Buddhist principles to his way of governing the people. He was always delighted to receive sutras and the relics of the Buddha from any monk returning from China. Due to his enthusiasm, Buddhism was firmly established as a national religion. Towards the end of his life, King Chinhung became a monk. named Popun, "Dharma Cloud" in his

old age and his wife became a nun at Yonghung-sa. (Several Shilla kings were ordained and their queens and families often followed the example and entered monasteries.)

The Arts

The arts flourished during the Shilla Period. A huge

Model of Hwangnyong-sa Temple.

Avalokitesvara(Naksan-saTemple)

temple, Hwangnyong-sa, was built and it became the center of Buddhism for Shilla.

There is a record which clearly demonstrates the position and excellency achieved by such a great king as Chinhung. It is the story of the three Buddha statues of Hwangnyong-sa!

The three statues were made in the 35th year of the reign of King Chinhung. They were cast from of 34,200 kilos of iron ore and gold which had been sent in a big vessel by the Indian King Asoka (r. 270-235 BCE) who, during his reign, unified most of India for the first time. There is a story about him which concerns the origin of the gold and iron.

One day, lamenting that he could not be born at the time of the Buddha, he tried to make a Buddha statue triad out of gold and iron. Three times he tried and each time he failed. So, thinking that the failure must be due to his bad karma, he decided to put all the gold and iron in a vessel with a letter, saying, "We hope that this metal can be used to make a triad in a country which has good karma." He sent the vessel carrying the gold, the iron, and the letter away. It went from country to country but the triad could not be made until the ship arrived in Shilla.

This story shows the strong connection between Shilla and Buddhism. It also suggests that King Chinhung was very powerful as he was able to make the triad that Asoka could not make.

This story shows the strong connection between Shilla and Buddhism. It also suggests that King Chinhung was very powerful as he was able to make the triad that Asoka could not make.

Political Organization

At the time of King Chinhung, Shilla was a politically and geophysically weak kingdom surrounded by the stronger kingdoms of Paekje and Koguryo. During the years of King Chinhung's reign, Shilla gained in territory and made political and religious reforms. Therefore, King Chinhung is considered to have been one of the greatest kings in Korean history.

We are also told that King Chinhung established the P'ungwoltto which was an organization for training young men. It was founded on Buddhist ideas and contributed to the settling of national thought. According to a stone monument, which is still standing today, the king was always accompanied by monks. Also the names of monks were written before the names of all government officials.

P'ungwoltto, Youth Organization

The P'ungwoltto was a system or organization established on a national level by King Chinhung. It provided much of the moral and military leadership necessary for Shilla in her drive to unify the peninsula. We find the story of the creation of this organization in the Samguk-sagi and Samguk-yusa.

Wonhwa

"King Chinhung chose beautiful girls and made the "Wonhwa," a record states. This was an organization to educate young girls in order to develop their talents; it was very important to the administration of the affairs of state. The king began with two girls, Nammo and Kyojong (or Chunjong) and soon each one had 300 followers. But Kyojong was jealous of Nammo and killed her. And when this murder was discovered, Nammo was put to death and the institution of "Wonhwa" was abolished.

Hwarang

"A few years after this event, King Chinhung again thought about the education of the young. This gave rise to the formation of the 'P'ungwoltto' for the prosperity of the nation. He ordered virtuous, superior and refined boys from good, aristocratic families to be chosen, and he made them 'hwarang,' or 'Flower Boys,' a name probably derived from the fact that the boys were beautifully decorated. Among these young men, Solwon was chosen to be the head of the group, or kuksson. This was the beginning of the hwarang, the members of the organization, and creation of the kuksson, the leader."

This P'ungwoltto has been wrongly called "hwarangdo" by many scholars who very carelessly misunderstood hwarang to be the center of the organization. However, the so-called hwarangdo did not have any authority: It is clearly recorded that this organization of young men formed by King Chinhung was called P'ungwoltto in the history books. Furthermore, some scholars have long considered the organization as consisting of warriors or soldiers. This, too, is wrong. It was an organization formed

He ordered virtuous, superior and refined boys from good, aristocratic families to be chosen, and he made them 'hwarang,' or 'Flower Boys,' a name probably derived from the fact that the boys were beautifully decorated.

*Roof-end
Tile With Monster
Mask.*

to train the youth purely in self- improvement and so that the nation might prosper. The organization consisted of a head, the kuksson, hwarang, and his followers, the nangdo, consisting of monks and laymen. The young men were usually from about 14-15 to 17-18 years of age. There were also monks who were much older than the boys called nangdo monks.

The kuksson was chosen from among the hwarang and he held a position of national authority, being the head of the organization, and was even respected by the king. He was considered as a symbol of Maitreya Buddha, the Future Buddha, and was treated as the little Buddha of the nation.

It is recorded that the boys were beautifully decorated with flowers and other ornaments. We can imagine that the reason for this came from the relationship between the hwarang and Maitreya who is always depicted wearing rich clothes and jewels. The monks, the nangdo, in the organization were under the kuksson and their prime function was to give guidance.

The hwarang lived according to Buddhist principles but, as they were warriors, they had slightly different precepts. (The adjustment of the precepts is very indicative of the effort Buddhism has always made to adapt to circumstances.)

1. Serve the king with loyalty.
2. Serve and tend parents with filial devotion.
3. Treat friends with sincerity.

He was considered as a symbol of Maitreya Buddha, the Future Buddha, and was treated as the little Buddha of the nation.

4. Do not retreat from battle fields.

5. Be discriminating about the taking of life.

There were two main influences on P'ungwoltto. One was the idea of the Chakravatin, the universal monarch and the other was the belief in Maitreya, the Future Buddha. These beliefs were very important to King Chinhung and so he named his two sons, Tongnyun, or "bronze wheel," and Kumnyun, or "gold wheel," proof of the influence of the concept of Chakravatin on the king. The hwarang were also known as the yonghwa-hyangdo, "Incense Group of the Dragon Flower," the followers of Maitreya. The Maitreya-sutra and the sutras mentioning the Chakravatin show that the Maitreya Buddha and the idea of Chakravatin were intimately interconnected.

It is interesting to note that incense was introduced from China during this period. The people, not knowing its use, thought it magical and so employed it for curing disease!

Buddhist Culture of the Three Kingdoms

The transmission of Buddhism to the Three Kingdoms brought significant development in many aspects of national culture. Before the advent of Buddhism, there was hardly any culture established on a national level. After the arrival of Buddhism, the arts flourished with the making of bells (the huge cast iron ones beautifully decorated with relief work to be seen at temples in Korea), pagodas, statues, carving, architecture, painting and industrial arts. Buddhism contributed to the development of the spiritual civilization greatly. But today, because of many invasions and the lack of careful preservation, only a few records exist. These consist of archaeological sites, historical remains and books.

Temples

The first Korean temples to be built, according to records, were Songmun-sa (or Ch'o-mun-sa) and Ibulran-sa. They were built in 375 by Koguryo King Sosurim. Koguryo King Kwang-gaet'o built nine temples in P'yongyang in 392. And other Koguryo temples like Kumgang-sa, Panyong-sa,

After the arrival of Buddhism, the arts flourished with the making of bells (the huge cast iron ones beautifully decorated with relief work to be seen at temples in Korea), pagodas, statues, carving, architecture, painting and industrial arts.

Temple Compound(Pulguk-sa temple)

Yongt' ap-sa, were also built very early on according to the records. Sadly, we know nothing about the form or style of these temples.

However, an ancient temple site, believed to be that of Kumgang-sa, was excavated at Ch' ong-am-ni, near P' yongyang and the Taedong-gang River in 1938. The arrangement of the temple compound seems to have been centered on an octagonal building. Traces of two other buildings are found to the east and west of the octagonal building. To the north, there are traces of a big building, and to the south a trace of a gate. Further north, there are traces of four more buildings, one quite separate from the rest.

A temple was built on Han-san as soon as Buddhism was brought to Paekje.

Later on, during the reign of kings Pop and Mu, Wanghung-sa and Miruk-sa were built respectively. In the record, some names of other temples such as Yoak-sa, Oham-sa, Ch' onwang-sa, Toyang-sa and Paeksok-sa were also mentioned. Some of these temples have been excavated but some remain to be dug. Wanghung-sa was a very magnificent temple in Puyo, the capital of Paekje at

Today, most
famous Korean
pagodas are made
of stone. But
originally, pagodas
were made of
wood, earth,
bricks, or other
materials.

that time. The site of Miruk-sa is the largest of the sites of Korean temples and it shows a unique arrangement of the three buildings.

Hungnyun-sa, which was finished in 545, the 5th year of the reign of King Chinhung, was probably the first and the largest Shilla temple. Yonghung-sa and Hwangnyong-sa were built at the same time as were Chiwon-sa and Shilje-sa. All of these temples were large and magnificent; many more were to be built as the years went by.

Such great temples influenced the architectural style and the building techniques used at that time enormously. In this way extraordinary developments occurred. Special roofs to cover the huge halls had to be created and the arrangement of beams to support the roofs required great engineering ability.

Pagodas

Today, most famous Korean pagodas are made of stone. But originally, pagodas were made of wood, earth, bricks, or other materials.

*Chongnim-sa Temple Site Pagoda
(Paekje, Nat'l Treasure No. 9)*

As far as the records show, the first pagoda to have been constructed was Yukwang-t'ap in Lia Tung in Koguryo. According to the Samguk-yusa the precise date of the construction of this pagoda is unknown. It was made of earth, and consisted of three parts, the top resembled a Korean traditional kettle turned upside down. A king (one record says it was a sage king, but it is not certain who the king was), after finding the earthen pagoda, built a seven-storey wooden pagoda out of devotion.

Another record tells of a stone pagoda at Yongt'ap-sa. A legend says that Master Podok found the pagoda under the ground following the instructions of a supernatural being. It had eight sides and seven stories.

Besides these few records, not much else is known about Koguryo pagodas. We do not know how many there were nor do we know their style.

According to Chinese records, Paekje had many temple pagodas. However, specific records of these pagodas are very rare. Among the existing stone pagodas, the oldest in Korea and largest in the east is on the site of Miruk-sa, together with the stupa of Chongnim-sa site, they show us the excellent technique and style of Paekje pagodas. In the making of pagodas in particular, Paekje had many great artists and so they were sent to Shilla.

One particular example is the Paekje artist Abiji who was sent to Shilla to help build the nine-storey, wooden pagoda at Hwangnyong-sa, the oldest, recorded, Shilla pagoda which was finished in 645. It stood 68 m. high and was outstandingly magnificent. The story of the building of this pagoda is recorded in Samguk-yusa. The Diamond Altar (actually made of stone) of T'ongdo-sa, where Master Chajang enshrined the Buddha's relics which he had received from Manjusri, and a pagoda of Taehwa-sa were built at the same time.

Master Chajang recommended the building of that first pagoda for the security of the nation. It was thought that such religious actions as the building of a pagoda would protect the nation against disasters and the nine neighboring, hostile countries including Japan and China. Pagodas were held to be lucky and also they were considered as able to "balance" or "mend" "wounds" in the earth. These are unlucky spots recognized by geomancers.

The present pagoda at Punhwang-sa is the oldest brick-shaped, stone pagoda among all those which were built before the unification of the peninsula in 668.

Statues

Most of the gold-plated, bronze Buddha statues which existed up to this time were from Koguryo and Paekje; the technique and beauty of these statues is wonderful. Paekje King Song, in 545 made a huge Buddha statue, wishing that all living beings in the world attain enlightenment. He also sent a Buddha statue to Japan when he introduced Buddhism there, following it later on

It was thought that such religious actions as the building of a pagoda would protect the nation against disasters and the nine neighboring, hostile countries including Japan and China.

Miruk-sa Temple site Pagoda
(Paekje, Nat'l Treasure No. 11)

with more, including Maitreyas. Even today, great Paekje Buddha statues such as Ma-aebul are occasionally discovered in the ground.

We have already seen that King Chinhung, in 574, made a Buddha triad for Hwangnyong-sa. This triad, together with the nine-storey pagoda and a jade belt received by King Chinp'yong from heaven are three national jewels of the Shilla period. Master Yangji, during the reign of Queen Sondok, made: a Buddha triad; the four temple guardian statues for Yongjo-sa; the arahant statues on eight sides under the pagoda of Ch'onwang-sa; and a Buddha triad and temple guardians for Popnim-sa. He also made roof tiles for the pagoda building of Yongjo-sa, as well as writing the Chinese characters on the boards of

Yongjo-sa and Popnim-sa. He built a brick pagoda and kept 3,000 Buddha statues at Sokjjang-sa where he lived. In this way Master Yangji did a lot for Buddhism as he was a master of making statues and pagodas, carving and painting. Legend says that he had supernatural powers.

Japan was helped by this flourishing culture of the Three Kingdoms Period. Paekje, in particular, sent many Buddha statues, including a stone Maitreya Buddha statue, and other Buddhist instruments. Moreover, all kinds of technicians and artists talented in such fields as the making Buddha statues, building temples, Buddhist paintings, and making roof tiles were sent to Japan. There they trained apprentices in their special talents so that the techniques could be handed down. Apart from Paekje, Koguryo also sent many artists to Japan. In particular, Master Tamjing excelled in painting so he taught the Japanese how to paint for the first time. And he also imparted techniques in making colors, paper and inkstones.

In the Three Kingdoms Period, there are many legends about pagodas and Buddha statues. Some tell that they were not made by human hands but that they appeared out of the earth or beneath some body of water, or that they came down from heaven. Some of the more famous legends include: a Koguryo pagoda at Yongt'ap-sa; a stone Maitreya Buddha statue at Saeng-ui-sa which was discovered in Samhwaryong pass by Master

Buddha Gilt Bronze
(Koguryo, Nat'l Treasure No. 119)

Seated Buddha(Maitreya) Traid, Shilla

Saeng-ui in the reign of Queen Sondok; Sabul-san, a big stone, of Taesung-sa which was "dropped" from heaven in 597 and had Tathagathas on four sides of it; and three Maitreya Buddha statues which rose up from a big spring on Yonghwa-san in the reign of King Mu.

Not only did the arts flourish, but there were many famous monks living at this time. One of the most celebrated in the entire history of Korea was Master Wonhyo. Here is one of the most celebrated stories about him. It is important because it led to his main, original contribution to Korean Buddhist philosophy and this development is still central to Korean Buddhism today.

> Not only did the arts flourish, but there were many famous monks living at this time. One of the most celebrated in the entire history of Korea was Master Wonhyo.

Masters Wonhyo and Uisang

Master Wonhyo (617-686), one of Korea's greatest scholars, was born in a simple family. After living as a monk for many years, he renounced religious life in order to better serve the people. Married for a short time to a princess, he had one son. As a scholar he wrote many important treatises in which he explained his philosophy of oneness, Ekayana, the interrelatedness of everything in the universe. The development of this view is due to an event in his life.

At the time that Master Wonhyo lived, many monks went to China to study and look for teachers. Wonhyo and his close friend, Uisang, also set out for China together; both of them wanted to study Buddhism there. One night on the way, Wonhyo awoke thirsty and, searching round, he found a container with delicious cool water in it. He drank the water and, his thirst quenched, he went back to sleep.

In the morning, he found that the vessel from which he had drunk was a skull.

Suddenly he saw that everything depends on the mind – thirsty, he had found the water so refreshing and the vessel so welcoming but on awakening, in the light of day, he was disgusted to find a dirty skull – and he attained enlightenment. Realizing that it was no longer necessary for him to go to China in search of a teacher, he returned home.

Master Uisang continued the journey. After ten years studying in China under a great master, Uisang offered a special gift to his teacher: a poem in the shape of seal which, when written down, geometrically represents infinity. This poem contained the essence of the Avatamsaka-sutra (an extremely long text explaining the universe); it is one of the greatest offerings of the Korean people to the world.

> **Suddenly he saw that everything depends on the mind - thirsty, he had found the water so refreshing and the vessel so welcoming but on awakening, in the light of day, he was disgusted to find a dirty skull – and he attained enlightenment.**

The Story of Wonhyo's Awakening

*Water-Moon
Avalokitesvara
(Koryo. 1310
Hanging Scroll,
Color on Silk)*

Buddhism from Unification until Today

United Shilla Period (668-935)

In 668 CE, Shilla conquered the other kingdoms and Buddhism became the central cultural force uniting the peninsula. This period came to be known as the United Shilla Period. Various rituals were developed and performed as spiritual requests for protection from foreign invasion which was seen to be a constant problem to the little peninsula standing between the two vastly larger civilizations of Japan and China. National sentiment was strong and the people worked hard for unity and understanding, with everything tending towards the realization of their patriotic aspirations. From the very start, the Buddhism studied used a unified approach, the "One Mind," the universal interrelatedness of everything, as taught by Wonhyo.

Throughout the United Shilla Period, Buddhism continued to prosper and grow, both academically and culturally. This was the time of the creation of some of the finest Korean art; the main temples of Korea were built; pagodas were erected; beautiful statues fashioned – all of this was of profound significance to the country's Buddhist heritage. The famous rock statue of the Buddha in Sokkur-am cave, in Kyongju, was carved in 732: today it still evokes a sense of wonder and is one of the items on the UNESCO World Heritage List.

The Avatamsaka-sutra and the Lotus Sutra were the main focus of study. Much of the chanting concentrated on Amitabha, the Buddha of Universal Light, and Avalokitesvara, the Bodhisattva of Compassion.

Towards the end of the United Shilla Period, the Chan School (Son in Korean, Zen in Japanese) was introduced from China and this added a new dimension to Korean

> Throughout the United Shilla Period, Buddhism continued to prosper and grow, both academically and culturally.

Buddhism. Meditation and direct experience were emphasized over concentration on studying the texts. Nine different schools emerged and they were known as the Nine Mountains of Son.

Koryo (935-1392)

After the glory of Shilla faded, the Koryo Dynasty assumed power in the 10th century. Buddhism continued to be the national religion, with the kings establishing shrines and temples throughout the country. However, excessive focus was placed on rituals and this created an unfavorable atmosphere for spiritual development.

Buddha, Iron(Koryo, Treasure No. 332)

In an attempt to purify and renew the spiritual aspect of Buddhism, several monks struggled against the ritualistic trend. One of these monks was Master Uich' on (1055-1101), son of King Munjong (1046-1083), who collected about 4,000 volumes of Buddhist texts while studying in China; from these the Tripitaka Koreana, the complete collection of Buddhist texts carved on wood blocks, was produced. This eminent Koryo monk emphasized the importance of bringing the contemplative, Zen, and Textual, Avatamsa, traditions together under a new school: he called it Ch' ont' ae. It was this development which brought new life to Koryo Buddhism.

Buddhism remained the dominant intellectual influence during the later years of Koryo, as Confucianism, introduced to the peninsula at the same time as Buddhism, had not yet gained much popularity.

Master Chinul (1158-1210), usually known as Pojo-kuksa, became the leading monk of Korea. He founded Songgwang-sa Temple on Mt. Chogye, and this large temple remained the headquarters of the Son sect for over 300 years. The Nine Schools of Son (Zen) were unified by Master T'aego (1301-82) under the name Chogye which has remained the main sect to this day.

Choson (1392-1910)

Buddhism remained the dominant intellectual influence during the later years of Koryo, as Confucianism, introduced to the peninsula at the same time as Buddhism, had not yet gained much popularity.

With the downfall of the Koryo Dynasty in 1392, Buddhism slowly declined as the new rulers of the Choson Dynasty adopted Neo-Confucianism. Prior to this, many Buddhist monks had become overly involved in politics, resulting in royal strife. The new interest in Confucianism led to the oppression and restriction of Buddhism by some Choson kings. Temples could not be built near towns and had to be constructed in the mountains; many temples were pulled down; monks were looked down on and, for many years, not permitted to enter the capital city. While some kings persecuted Buddhism, the common people continued to go to the temples. Scholars, too, frequented the temples.

At the beginning of the Choson Dynasty, geomancers were consulted in order to find the ideal site for a new capital. They chose an ancient place called "Hanyang" which was then renamed "Seoul" and which has been the center of culture and learning for the peninsula since that time. The name means "capital" in Korean and was probably derived from the ancient Indian place most dear to the Buddha: Sravasti. In Chinese, "Sravasti" became "Sarobol" and finally "Seoul" in Korean.

In the late 16th century, during the Japanese invasion by the armies of Hideyoshi, Buddhism came to the country's rescue. At the age of 72, Master Sosan (1520-1604) and his disciple Samyong (1544-1610), trained and led a band of 5,000 Buddhist monks against the Japanese troops who had invaded the peninsula and won. For a short time, the persecution of Buddhism was reduced because the government was grateful to the monks who had saved the country. Following the defeat of the

Master So-san

Hideyoshi Invasion, Master Samyong, was sent as chief delegate to Japan and in 1604 he completed a peace treaty.

Modern Times: Renewal

In 1910, the Choson Dynasty came to an end with the annexation of the country to Japan. During the Colonial Period, Buddhism was greatly favored and supported by Japanese policies. However, the celibate sects were discouraged and monks were encouraged to take wives, following Japanese custom. Also, contrary to tradition, the heads of temples were appointed by the Japanese occupation authorities.

Unfortunately, during this period, many Buddhist art treasures were taken to Japan. Today the Buddhists, in co-operation with the Korean government, are negotiating with Japan in order to have these stolen treasures returned.

After Liberation in 1945, the celibate ordained members of the main sect of Korean Buddhism, Chogye, superseded the married monks who had taken over the principle temples during the Japanese Occupation. Large numbers of men and women were ordained and there was a great revival of Korean Buddhism.

Recently, many new temples and centers have opened in the towns. Programs for people of all ages include: learning to chant, studying of texts, all night meditation classes, social gatherings. About half the population of Korea is Buddhist as many people still see it as old fashioned to call themselves Buddhists and do not own up to the fact. In addition, most Koreans, even though they may not call themselves Buddhists, maintain a Buddhist view of life and the afterworld. Those who follow other religions keep many customs which are Buddhist in origin and everyone knows that Korean culture is primarily rooted in Buddhism.

*Buddhist Mass
Meeting for Renewal*

The History from another Perspective

(This article appeared as the introduction to the second book, Buddhist Thought in Korea, in a series on Korean Buddhism published by the Korean Buddhist Research Institute of Dongguk University Press. It is written by Professor Lee Pong-chun and offers a different, interesting perspective on the history of Korean Buddhism.

One point must be clarified. All through the history of Korean Buddhism, there was a gentle rivalry between the approach based on academic study and that of practice, meditation, only. Two separate factions were usually clearly discernable. The reconciliation of these two was the wish of many of the great masters such as Master Wonhyo. In order to make this clear, we have chosen to use capitalized Study (Academic) and Meditation when mentioning the schools or factions as opposed to the activity.)

Originally, Buddhism was introduced to Korea as a foreign thought system. Growing up in India and coming to Korea through Central Asia and China, the initial phase of introduction and the subsequent integration was difficult and only slowly did Korean Buddhism emerge and a new development take place. This then became the ideological foundation and cultural backdrop of the Korean people, influencing every stage of history and every aspect of culture. The process of the creation of Korean Buddhism was, like the development of Buddhist culture in other countries, the welding together of the teachings of the Buddha with the indigenous culture. Thus Koreans added their own characteristics to the basic Buddhism which they received, creating a totally new form of Buddhism which differs from that of India and that of China.

The individuality and unique characteristics of Korean Buddhism are seen through the whole of Korean culture.

Thus Koreans added their own characteristics to the basic Buddhism which they received, creating a totally new form of Buddhism which differs from that of India and that of China.

In particular they are vividly confirmed in the tracing of the development of Korean Buddhist thought. This overview of the Buddhist philosophical trends will help the reader to understand the overall process and the main characteristics which have persisted throughout the evolution of the development of Korean Buddhism: The Process of Philosophical Development

Ever since its introduction to the peninsula, Korean Buddhist thought has undergone various stages in its evolution. These are summarized as follows:

a) Period of Introduction: the initial contact and subsequent adjustment;

b) Period of Settlement: the beginning of Hinayana and Mahayana studies in the Three Kingdoms Period;

c) Period of Expansion: enlargement and development of various fields of Mahayana studies in the middle Shilla Period;

d) Period of Spreading: introduction of Zen in the late Shilla Period and encouragement of Buddhist studies in the early Koryo Period;

e) Period of Transfiguration: development of community movements and acceptance of Linchi (Kor. Imje; Jap. Rinzai) Zen in the late Koryo Period;

f) Period of Stagnation: oppression of Buddhism in the early Choson Period;

g) Period of Taking a New Direction: union of Zen and Academic study and three approaches of practice after the middle Choson Period.

The above divisions are purely arbitrary and defined for convenience's sake. However, they do trace the process of development through the different periods of history and so delimit the advancement of Korean Buddhist thought. Let us now briefly examine the content of Buddhist thought in conformity with each period.

The Period of Introduction

After its initial introduction in 372 CE, Buddhism was

> However, they do trace the process of development through the different periods of history and so delimit the advancement of Korean Buddhist thought.

> Buddhism was welcomed and supported by the kings and royal families of the Three Kingdoms because it could offer a more useful governing ideology for social development, compared to the original system of thinking and culture.

Contemplative Bodhisattva (Three Kingdoms Period)

faced with the problem of settling into a new environment. The socio-philosophical milieu of the time was centered on Shamanism. Accordingly, the main task of Buddhism, as is the case with any new religion, was to try to educate the people by inspiration and sometimes the use of miracles. The main principles of Buddhist teaching were then offered to the people. These consisted mainly of the teachings of karma and cause and effect. So that Buddhism developed its philosophy in Korea centering around the theory of karma, which is a basic doctrine of Buddhism, and this tenet alone reformed the primary Shamanistic culture. The existing gods were naturally assimilated into Buddhism and the foundation was set. Buddhism was welcomed and supported by the kings and royal families of the Three Kingdoms because it could offer a more useful governing ideology for social development, compared to the original system of thinking and culture. It was seen as a much needed element around which the confrontation of the Three Kingdoms could take place. For they were all eager to be the focal point of unification and centralization. Accordingly, Buddhism was accepted by royal families and aristocrats and then it gradually developed into a national system.

The Period of Settlement

As a result of the usefulness with which Buddhism was perceived, it was able to settle into Korea not long after its introduction. It is hard to pinpoint the exact time of this settlement, but it can be considered to be one or two centuries after the initial contact. With establishment came the impetus for a high level of Buddhist research and development, from about the early 6th century. The research carried out at this time was into purely doctrinal questions which were not related to the national trend in Buddhist thought and it was this development which is seen as proof of the final amalgamation of Korean Buddhism into Korean culture. Existing

Incense Burner Gilt-bronze.
(Paekje, Nat'l Treasure No. 287)

Korean records of the research carried out at this time are very few but the trends and outlines can be considered from Chinese records dating from that period.

According to these records, the research of scholar-monks of the Koguryo Kingdom - which accepted Buddhism initially - was most active. Koguryo Master Sungnang systematically researched and developed the study of the Three Treatises, that is, Chung-non (Mulamadhyamika-karika-sastra, Treatise on the Middle), Shibimun-non (Dvadasanikaya-sastra, Treatise on the Twelve Gates), and Paeng-non (Cathusataka, Treatise in One Hundred Verses), which are fundamental texts of Indian Buddhism, especially Mahayana Madhyamika philosophy. Hence he directly influenced the establishment of the Chinese School of the Three Treatises. Besides him, many Koguryo masters were active either in China or in Koguryo. Master Chihwang studied the philosophy of Sarvastivada, a major branch of Hinayana Buddhism, Master Podok is known to have been a great scholar of Yolban-kyong (Nirvana-sutra), and Master P'ayak studied Ch'ont'ae (Ch. T'ien-t'ai).

In Paekje there was also a lot of research carried out. After Master Kyomik returned from a pilgrimage to India in 526, research and writing on Vinaya philosophy was especially popular, and belief in the Lotus Sutra and

Standing Medicine Buddha.
(Shilla, Nat'l Treasure No. 28)

Maitreya, the Future Buddha, increased dramatically. The doctrinal study of Paekje, which introduced Buddhism to Japan, became the foundation of Japanese Buddhism.

Shilla recognized Buddhism officially later than Koguryo and Paekje. Belief in the Pure Land of Maitreya was eagerly accepted as a kind of governing Buddhist ideology from the beginning. Later, from the early 7th century, studies on various Mahayana texts such as sutras and Mahayana vinayas became popular. The Buddhist thought of the Three Kingdoms does not seem to have gone much beyond research into the texts of Hinayana and Mahayana. But Koguryo Master Sungnang's study of the Three Treatises is considered the origin of Korean Buddhist philosophy. Because of this, only some of the studies of this period are selectively seen to be important.

The Period of Expansion

After the middle 7th century, Korean Buddhist thought developed greatly but this growth was very different from the early days. For about 130 years from the time King Munmu (r. 661-681) who unified the Three Kingdoms in 668 and King Hyegong (r. 765-780), research into the Mahayana was very active and many books were written. The research of this period was varied enough to cover most fields of Buddhist studies such as Vinaya, Three Treatises, Vijnanamatravada (Kor. Yushik), Avatamsa (Kor. Hwaom), Esoteric, Maitreya and the Pure Land. But especially Avatamsa philosophy developed by masters Uisang and Wonhyo formed the main focus of study. In addition, the Vijnanamatravada study of

Master Wonch'uk and succeeding Shilla masters occupied an important place in Buddhist research of the time.

Master Uisang continued in the line of orthodox Chinese Avatamsa study, and after his return from China, he devoted himself to advocating Avatamsa doctrines and establishing the tradition of Shilla Avatamsa. Master Wonhyo made a comprehensive study of Hinayana and Mahayana, and developed very creative, innovative theories on the philosophy of the Awakening of Faith centered around the idea of the tathagatagarbha (Tathagata's womb) and the theory that everything arises from the mind. Such philosophy as that of the Awakening of Faith shares a mutual understanding with Avatamsa philosophy, hence Master Wonhyo is also considered to be an established Avatamsa philosopher. The Avatamsa philosophy advocated by these masters corresponded well to the socio-political integration which was required for Shilla to head for unification.

However, Shilla Vijnanamatravada philosophy which, along with the Three Treatises philosophy, is one of the representative trends of Mahayana study, originated from Master Wonch'uk who studied in T'ang. Master Wonch'uk greatly contributed to the new Vijnanamatravada study which was introduced to China from India by Chinese Master Hsuan-tsang. Master Wonch'uk's Vijnanamatravada philosophy is well known in the context of its confrontation with that of Master K'uei-chi who was also a disciple of Master Hsuan-tsang. Master Wonch'uk's philosophy was inherited by Shilla masters and it was the point of departure for more active research. Apart from all the other fields of Mahayana studies such as Pure Land, Esoteric Buddhism, research into the Lotus Sutra, and belief in Avalokitesvara, this new direction developed enough to attract close attention in the middle Shilla Period.

The Period of Spreading Out

But the above research met limits of development in the late Shilla Period. Exegetic studies replaced the earlier research which gave rise to new philosophy and theory,

> Master Uisang continued in the line of orthodox Chinese Avatamsa study, and after his return from China, he devoted himself to advocating Avatamsa doctrines and establishing the tradition of Shilla Avatamsa.

and exceptional writing, as was previously common, was hardly ever produced. Shilla Buddhism needed fresh stimulation and a new impetus to get it going again. This new dimension, one which differed radically from existing trends, was introduced by Shilla masters who had studied in China. It was Son (Ch. Chan, Jap. Zen, hereafter Zen). In particular, it came in the form of the Hung-chou School of Master Ma-tsu Tao-i (709-788), which can be traced to the Sixth Chinese Zen patriarch, Hui-neng (638-713), which denied all ideological studies, such as Avatamsa, and emphasized on sitting meditation. This dealt a powerful blow to the formal, scholastic schools of Buddhism which had fallen into the habit of dry academic pursuits.

During the Koryo Dynasty (918-1392), Zen philosophy was fully accepted and developed greatly. The founder of the Koryo Dynasty, King T'aejo, eagerly supported the movement and summoned many Zen masters who could be useful to the management of his new kingdom. Accordingly, after the foundation of Koryo, various philosophies overwhelmed current Buddhist studies, even though Koryo Buddhism intended to follow the tradition of Shilla Buddhism in principle. Therefore, the Shilla Buddhist studies carried out after the middle period were continued into Koryo and formed the basis of the new direction taken. Thus there was diversity in the studies. These included: Avatamsa philosophy and Yogacara and Vijnanamatravada philosophy were newly develop along with the sudden rise of Zen; Vinaya, Esoteric Buddhism and Shinin or thought of the Divine Seal evolved; and Ch'ont'ae (Ch. T'ien-t'ai) study suddenly became important.

Roof-end Tile With Smiling Face.

The founder of the Koryo Dynasty, King T'aejo, eagerly supported the movement and summoned many Zen masters who could be useful to the management of his new kingdom.

Master Uich' on
adopted a new
tendency of
Chinese Avatamsa,
and proclaimed the
theory of dual
practice of study
and meditation,
that is, that
doctrinal studies
and actual practice
should be carried
out together.

Avatamsa was still the most representative study of the Koryo Period. Master Kyunyo (923-973) inherited the Avatamsa philosophy of Shilla Master Uisang and developed his own Avatamsa theory of "reconciliation of nature and characteristics." Master Kyunyo's Avatamsa philosophy was criticized by Master Uich' on (1055-1101) being biased in its view on doctrines. Master Uich' on adopted a new tendency of Chinese Avatamsa, and proclaimed the theory of dual practice of study and meditation, that is, that doctrinal studies and actual practice should be carried out together. Master Uich' on, on the other hand, went one step further and established the Koryo Ch' ont' ae School from the standpoint of dual practice of study and meditation.

It was at this time that the Ch' ont' ae doctrine and meditation, which had been studied from the early Koryo Period, became the main stream of the new philosophy. Besides Avatamsa and Ch' ont' ae, Yuga and Vijnanamatravada also became prominent from the reign of King Hyonjong (r. 1009-1031). But Master Sohyon (1038-1096), during the reign of King Munjong, did not continue in the tradition of Shilla Vijnanamatravada which had originated from Master Wonch' uk, but he turned towards the Vijnanamatravada philosophy of Chinese Master K' uei-chi, which claimed to be orthodox Chinese Vijnanamatravada.

*Vairocana Buddha
(Koryo, 11th Century)*

The Period of Transfiguration

The rapid development of Ch' ont' ae philosophy influenced the whole of Buddhist studies in the early Koryo Period. Especially the Zen School was deeply affected. The result was that many Zen masters moved to the new Ch' ont' ae School. This shows that the Ch' ont' ae philosophy of Master Uich' on who claimed that the dual practice of study and meditation was necessary, had absorbed Zen philosophy. The result was that the hitherto active Zen made poor progress once the Ch' ont' ae School was founded.

It was Master Chinul (1158-1210) of the middle Koryo Period who overcame the hardships of Zen and created a fresh direction in the Zen tradition. He fiercely criticized the existing Buddhist communities like the Avatamsa School which revealed excessive political interests and conspiracy with aristocrats on the one hand, and developed community movements centered around Zen in local places far from the capital, Kae-gyong, aimed at renovating Buddhism on the other hand. His Meditation and Wisdom Community emphasized the equal, balanced practice of meditation and wisdom in order to keep the religious purity of Buddhism from the pollution of political power. At the same time, it was aimed at the study of all aspects of

Master Chinul

Zen. Master Chinul's intentions are well seen through his creative Zen philosophy of the three approaches: the approach of "equal maintenance of alertness and calmness," the approach of "complete and sudden faith and understanding," and the "shortcut" approach. His creative Zen attitude forms a good contrast to that of Uich'on who intended to include Zen in the Academic School by founding the Koryo Ch'ont'ae School.

When the Koryo Zen tradition was again roused from stagnation and stimulated by Master Chinul's community movement, the Ch'ont'ae School founded a similar community. Called the White Lotus Community, it was created by Master Yose (1163-1245) and based in a local temple. Master Yose developed three approaches to repentance as taught in the Lotus Sutra as well as emphasizing the wish to be reborn in the Pure Land and the Ch'ont'ae practice of Concentration and Insight. In that way he advocated popular Buddhism which made this movement different from Master Uch'on's Ch'ont'ae philosophy. The White Lotus Community together with Master Chinul's community affirm the philosophical change of Buddhism in the middle Koryo Period.

Then a new tradition of Zen was introduced from Yuan in the late Koryo Period. It was at the time when military rule, which had been encouraged in order to fight against the Mongols, was over and imperial rule was restored. Hence from the 13th century, Koryo's internal affairs were intervened upon by Yuan, and Koryo Buddhism found itself in a new situation: the new Chaun School and the Ch'ont'ae School coming from another lineage became active. However this was merely a social influence and not one that affected the philosophical movement at all. In fact it was the direct result of aristocratic Buddhism which had taken up a position closer to politics.

At that time, Ch'ont'ae Master Unmuk of the White Lotus Community persisted in his wish for the purification of folk Buddhism, and so he advocated having deep belief in Amitabha. Also Avatamsa Master Ch'ewon inspired belief in Kwanum (Avalokitesvara) based on the Flower Garland Sutra. In addition, one Master Wonch'an, of unknown origin, formed a peculiar esoteric group which practiced the pure conduct of reciting mantras and prognosticating rebirth in the Pure

It was Master Chinul (1158-1210) of the middle Koryo Period who overcame the hardships of Zen and created a fresh direction in the Zen tradition.

*Stone Buddha
(Koryo, Treasure No. 96)*

Land. What was common to the above tendencies was that they all relied on other power, that is the help of the Bodhisattvas or Buddhas, a very different trend from that of Zen.

It was in the middle of the 14th century, that Zen was introduced from Yuan by masters Po-u, Hyegun, and Kyonghan. The Zen School was one of five Chinese Zen families of the seven Chinese Zen schools. This family tradition was more active than any other. Zen prospered greatly in Koryo and an effort was made at reviving and renovating Zen Buddhist thought through this new direction. From the time of the development of the community movement by masters Chinul and Yose until the flourishing of Zen was a period of transfiguration for Korean Buddhist thought.

The Period of Stagnation

From the late 14th century on, the Choson Dynasty (1392-1910) which was founded on the political ideology of Neo-Confucianism, oppressed Buddhism and caused it to fall into stagnation. The second Choson king, T'aejong (r. 1400-1418), started implementing a strong policy of suppression and control so that Buddhism economically and culturally began to be destroyed. This harsh policy was enforced with political or socio-economic reasons in mind rather than any philosophical reasons. Therefore in spite of the general trend of persecution, some kings and members of the royal household personally followed Buddhism and had relationships with monks. Thus oppression and encouragement of Buddhism were both practiced during the Choson Dynasty.

The Period of Taking a New Direction

The variation of the oppression and encouragement policy towards Buddhism ended after the middle of the Choson Period. In the earlier part of the dynasty, Buddhist thought and belief had some influence on the general trend of events. But Neo-Confucian scholars led the Korean

Zen prospered greatly in Koryo and an effort was made at reviving and renovating Zen Buddhist thought through this new direction.

academic community and they became more and more powerful from the middle period on. Accordingly, Buddhism which had to survive in the mountains from the time of King Chungjong (r. 1506-1544) had a more urgent task in merely existing than it did in developing any new thought. Therefore Buddhism tried hard to find a way to harmonize Confucianism and Buddhism.

In an effort to reconcile the differences and put an end to the conflict, various books were written. Master Kihwa clearly states this intention in his Hyonjong-non written in the early period. The book was aimed at putting an end to Confucian scholars' misunderstanding of Buddhism and informing them of the true meaning. It was a kind of philosophical confrontation of the Confucian theory of the reasons for the rejection of Buddhism, but the conclusion was about the harmonization of Confucianism and Buddhism. Another book by an anonymous writer, Yusok-chirui-ron, was written with the same purpose in view and therefore contains the same material. Master Po-u's theory of "one right" was developed for the same purpose and it concerned the "one" as a universal principle and the "right" as an ethical principle. Through these means different master worked to harmonize Confucianism and Buddhism.

Efforts at reconciliation continued. Master Sosan Hyujong who led the Buddhist community of the middle Choson Period, tried hard to bring about peace. In his Son-ga-kui-gam (Paragon of Zen Family), he advocated the reconciliation of the three teachings, Confucianism, Buddhism, and Taoism. The task of Buddhism, which had been the union of Meditation and Study up to the middle of the Koryo Period, became the harmonization of Confucianism and Buddhism in Choson Dynasty.

In spite of all these negative influences, the Buddhist philosophical tendency of the early Choson Period moved forward. Though eight Meditation Schools and various Study Schools were amalgamated into two, Meditation and Study, by force, Zen and Ch'ont'ae communities were still active, and Zen philosophy was constantly trying to embrace Study. Besides, the project of writing Korean Buddhist texts, translation from Chinese into Korean was continued by kings Sejong and Sejo who actively encouraged Buddhism. The project

Master Po-u's theory of "one right" was developed for the same purpose and it concerned the "one" as a universal principle and the "right" as an ethical principle. Through these means different master worked to harmonize Confucianism and Buddhism.

was magnificent in scale, and it had an important philosophical meaning as well. The main Mahayana texts involved were: Surangama-sutra, Lotus Sutra, Diamond Sutra, and Heart Sutra. In addition, esoteric Buddhist texts, and various Zen texts were also published in han-gul, the new Korean script which King Sejong had invented. The extensive publication of these traditional Study texts is proof that, even though Choson Buddhism was mainly concerned with Meditation, Study also played an important role.

The project was of further importance because of the use of han-gul which was only employed by the masses and innovative Buddhist monks and supporters. This was of special interest as it attests to the popularization of Buddhism. In spite of these events, Buddhism was mainly oppressed and suffered greatly under the persecution of the government.

The policy continued without change after the middle period. However then there was also a new trend in Buddhist thinking. Now, the main task of the Choson Buddhist community became the transmission of Dharma lineages. That is, whereas the interpretation of Study from the standpoint of Meditation was prominent in the early period, the so-called theory of "throwing up Study and entering Meditation" became pervasive in the late period, hence the system of Dharma transmission appeared. But this does not indicate the absolute disappearance of the Study approach. Traditional Study systems like Avatamsa, Lotus Flower, Pure Land, and Esoteric Buddhism still continued. Besides these, Zen accepted Avatamsa especially the Madhyamika School and Pure Land chanting, even though Zen finally intended to resolve the other thoughts into itself. As a result, the unique phenomenon of the simultaneous practice of the three approaches, that is, Zen meditation, studying texts, and esoteric chanting was followed in the late Choson Period.

The above phenomena of Dharma transmission and the practicing of the three approaches was the Buddhist way of existence under the attack of the government. All official religious activities of Buddhism were blocked and so in order for anything to take place, it had to be done in the seclusion of the mountains. It was inevitable that the

Master Sosan Hyujong who led the Buddhist community of the middle Choson Period, tried hard to bring about peace. In his Son-ga-kui-gam (Paragon of Zen Family), he advocated the reconciliation of the three teachings, Confucianism, Buddhism, and Taoism.

Buddhist community could only be sustained by way of the Zen transmission of Dharma lineages. Also it was only natural for a community which had already lost its own particular characteristics to practice various doctrinal teachings such as Avatamsa, Pure Land, esoteric and belief in Avalokitesvara simultaneously.

But the above attitude, besides being a method of handling historical hardship, can be understood as the establishment of a new philosophical direction which was holistic. In fact, it is not excessive to say that Korean Buddhist thought has pursued a holistic approach ever since the time of its introduction right up to the present moment. Though Buddhist thought from the middle to late Choson periods was formed under the stress of oppression, it, too, was holistic. This is the reason that the middle and the late Choson periods are here described as the time during which a new direction in the sense of further development was created.

This, then, is most of the important information on the history of Korean Buddhism. Now we will pass on to a brief consideration of some of the features which make Korean Buddhism unique.

Buddha and Bodhisattvas(Choson)

FEATURES OF KOREAN BUDDHISM

FEATURES OF KOREAN BUDDHISM

Divine Bell of King Song-dok (Nat'l Treasure No. 29)

The Characteristics of Korean Buddhist Thought

Throughout its long history, certain attributes are almost always evident in Korean Buddhism. These are interesting to identify because they offer a whole picture. For, whatever the period or stage of development, there have always been certain prominent factors which affected the general Buddhist climate and so the culture and the people of the country.

Individuality

Korean Buddhist thought is basically closely related to the philosophical thinking of Chinese Buddhism. Therefore the initial Buddhism to be intro-duced was directly or indirectly Chinese and it was the new research done by Korean masters which created what came to be called Korean Buddhism. This was a form of Buddhism which was different from Chinese Buddhism, even though some of the basic ideas were Chinese in origin.

In Koguryo, Master Sungnang's research on the Three Treatises become the foundation of the Chinese Three Treatises School. Another example of individual development is to be seen in Shilla Vijnanamatravada which also developed apart from the teachings in China. Thus Vijnanamatravada followed the teachings of Shilla Master Wonch'uk who advocated a different view from his comrade, Chinese Master K'uei-chi. In the case of Paekje Vinaya thought, Paekje Master Kyomik had already introduced the original Indian vinayas in five parts one century earlier than the foundation of Chinese Vinaya School during the T'ang Dynasty. The Vinaya texts were translated in Paekje and published in 72 volumes, so that an individual Vinaya thought, one suited to the Paekje social system, was established. Master Uisang's Avatamsa thought is also very different from his Chinese Dharma friend Master Fa-tsang. Whereas Master Fa-tsang attached weight to the philosophical under-standing of Avatamsa doctrine, Master Uisang emphasized the practical part of Avatamsa centered around the idea of Ocean-seal Samadhi. Master Wonhyo also developed Avatamsa thought with his unique theory on the Awakening of Faith, without any Chinese influence.

Such original thinking and development of Korean Buddhism is again revealed in the introduction of Zen and its establishment in the late Shilla Dynasty. Shilla masters introduced Zen Dharma from various Chinese Zen schools, but they never proclaimed to belong to those schools. Instead, they either founded their own or joined the already existing Korean Nine Mountains of Zen and so held on to the Korean Zen tradition. This tendency is also seen in the Zen thought of Master Chinul in the middle Koryo Period. To devise a method of harmonization of Meditation and Study, he formed his own very individual Zen thought. To this end he accepted orthodox Chinese Zen thought on the one hand and quoted other studies like the

Korean Buddhist thought is basically closely related to the philosophical thinking of Chinese Buddhism.

Avatamsa theory of Li T'ung-hsuan – which is considered a non-orthodox Chinese Avatamsa School – on the other hand.

The holistic Buddhist practice of three approaches, meditation, studying sutras, and chanting in the period of forming a new direction can be seen as one example of the individuality of Korean Buddhism. This is due to the fact that, though it was a phenomenon which appeared in the process of overcoming problems, it certainly was a conclusion derived from Korean Buddhist thought which differed from its Chinese counterpart. In this way we can conclude that Korean Buddhist thought, in close connection with Chinese Buddhist thought, has firmly established its own individual identity.

Three-storied stone pagodas on Kamun-sa temple site.

Mental Foundation and Ideology

Korean Buddhism offered a mental framework and ideology which corresponded to each phase of social development in the historical process. The important task of Buddhism in the initial period of introduction was the problem of establishment. Buddhism embraced the primitive thinking of Shamanism and so developed traditional thinking. Concepts such as the theory of karma replaced Shamanistic belief, hence it brought about social development and functioned as a prop and strengthener of the sovereign power. All the Three Kingdoms made Buddhist thought their central ideology. Especially Shilla before unification of the peninsula, made the best use of Buddhism, letting it influence every aspect of life so that the culture developed greatly. The ideology which was particularly popular was the Pure Land of Maitreya. Examples are the Shilla thought of Sankha, the universal monarch (Chakravatin) and the system of P'ungwoltto, the organization for training young men called hwarang.

The Shilla kingdom went one step further. There Buddhist thought was used as a pivot point for the accomplishment of the unification of the Three Kingdoms and then it was taken as the foundation ideology of the new unified state. Buddhism, especially Avatamsa philosophy, then became very influential as a socio-political ideology for the reconciliation and the integration which were needed by Unified Shilla. The foundation ideology of Koryo was also based on Buddhist philosophy. The theory of reconciliation of Confucianism and Buddhism in the Choson Period, was an active effort made to overcome the ideological gap of the time.

Philosophical Reformation Movement

Korean Buddhist thought devoted itself to philosophical reformation and the overcoming of fixed concepts from the beginning. Just after becoming thoroughly established, Korean Buddhism entered a phase of philosophical settlement already at the time of the Three Kingdoms and immediately began to make full use of the research being carried out. This openness and willingness to receive new thinking shows the reformation oriented character; this trend continued throughout the history, long after the period of establishment.

After unification, Buddhist philosophy

was on a different level and Mahayana philosophy became fully developed. For it was not possible for the philosophy to stagnate at the level where it satisfied social ethics and sovereign ideology. And then once again, when Mahayana Buddhist philosophy met the limit of its conceptual development, Zen, which denies conceptual Buddhist thought, was introduced. It was a philosophical reformation movement. Encouragement of Buddhist studies in the early Koryo Period was done with the same view in mind. Thus Koryo masters did not merely continue the traditional thought system of Shilla Buddhism. They imported and integrated new thinking from Chinese studies. The community movements after the middle Koryo Period and the introduction of Zen in the later Koryo Period show stronger characteristics of philosophical reformation.

Pursuit of Harmonization and Unification

The pursuit of harmony and unification were constant focal points of Korean Buddhism. This is most remarkable in the history of Korean Buddhist thought, and it originated from Shilla Master Wonhyo's Buddhist thought. His whole thinking is centered on the idea of reconciliation. Through his creative theory, he harmonized the two different Buddhist values of categories of reality and ordinary categories which had been considered a problem. Also, he brought together the concept of the "void"(of Madhyamika philosophy) and that of "existence"(of Vijnanamatravada philosophy) - a subject of argument in Indian and Chinese studies - in the structure of his concept of the "One Mind."

> **Through his creative theory, he harmonized the two different Buddhist values of categories of reality and ordinary categories which had been considered a problem.**

This characteristic of harmonization and unification is also seen in the Vijnanamatravada thought of Master Wonch'uk and the Avatamsa thought of Master Uisang. Even more so, we find this dimension in the writings of Master Uich'on whose theory of dual practice of study and meditation aimed at the harmonization of doctrinal theories and actual practice, and so the unification of Meditation and Study which were in great conflict at that time. Master Chinul's Zen thought is the same. He boldly accepted Study, especially Avatamsa, which had been denied by the Meditation Schools and by that act he brought Meditation and Study together. Once again in the Zen thought of Master Sosan, during the Choson Dynasty when Buddhism was being persecuted, Confucianism, Taoism and Buddhism were brought together.

These trends of individuality, ideological foundation, reformation, and harmonization continue today. With 16 centuries of history behind it, Korean Buddhism now has a big responsibility to continue in the same vein. Korean Buddhist thought and culture are the ideological foundation of the Korean people and the driving force behind the development of the country. Today as much as ever, Korean Buddhism is Korean history. Therefore Buddhism is now being strongly urged to once again bring a fresh philosophical ideology and way of practice applicable to modern society.

The Orders

The Main Order: Chogye

The name of Korea's main sect, Chogye, comes from the mountain in China on which the Sixth Patriarch, Hui-neng (638-713), lived. The name "Chogye" was probably brought back from China by Master Toui in about 820 CE. It is an order which stresses meditation, originating from the Chan teachings of China. Slowly, many different Zen sects formed in Korea. Master T'aego (1301-82), a great monk, returned from China in 1346. After that he united all the Zen sects and called the resultant order "Chogye."

During the Choson Dynasty, when Buddhism was not favored, the Chogye Order continued to exist but with less force than before. After the Japanese colonization of Korea in 1910, the Chogye Order received yet another blow: married monks were introduced and Korean monks were encouraged to take wives.

It was only after liberation in 1945, in an age often referred to as the era of purification, that Korean Buddhism once again began to flourish. Public support grew and most of the large temples were once again run by the celibate monks of the Chogye Order.

The Chogye Order emphasizes meditation which is considered by most Buddhists to be the best way to attain enlightenment. The most venerated texts are: the Heart Sutra, the Diamond Sutra, the Platform Sutra of the Sixth Patriarch, the Avatamsaka Sutra, and the stories of ancient Zen Masters. There are 1,632 (1997) temples belonging to the Chogye Order; this does not include numerous little hermitages dotted about the mountainous areas. These temples are organized into twenty-five geographical regions; each region has a main temple. Of the twenty-five main temples, there are four major temples: T'ongdo-sa Temple, Haein-sa Temple, Songgwang-sa Temple, and Sudok-sa Temple. These four temples have a meditation hall and a major monks' training center within the same compound.

The scale of operation of the Chogye Order has been renewed and enlarged since 1986. The Buddhist newspaper published by the Chogye Order has an increased irculation. Monks are assigned to the military to serve soldiers, and teachers have been sent to Korean Buddhist centers established in countries such as United States, Japan, Hong Kong, Australia, and Europe. Now there is a radio station and TV

The Chogye Order emphasizes meditation which is considered by most Buddhists to be the best way to attain enlightenment. The most venerated texts are: the Heart Sutra, the Diamond Sutra, the Platform Sutra of the Sixth Patriarch, the Avatamsaka Sutra, and the stories of ancient Zen Masters.

network which function in collaboration with the Chogye Order. The Order consists of about 12,000 ordained members. There are 8.1 million active registered lay members and many, many more who are not registered (1997).

Other Orders

There are many other Buddhist sects in Korea. Although they share identical philosophy, the teachings of the Buddha, they differ in the area on which they lay stress and in the choice of principle text. All are Mahayana sects and some incorporate tantric influences into their teaching. The second largest sect is T'aego. The Hwaom, Chonghwa and Wonhyo sects all stress the Flower Garland Sutra, Avatamsaka. The

Pophwa, Purip and Ilsung, among others, concentrate on the Lotus Sutra. The Pure Land sect venerates the Lotus Sutra and the Pomun is the only all women Buddhist sect in the world.

Most of the Korean Buddhists sects were founded after the liberation from the Japanese in 1945. Since then Korean Buddhism has been changing rapidly: programs have been more diversified and education has been emphasized. Country and mountain temples have been attracting more and more people. Increasingly there are also more Buddhist places to go to in the cities. (In the past, during the persecution of Buddhism in the Choson Dynasty, temples were not allowed to be built in the cities.) Another activity is the translation of Buddhist texts from Chinese into Korean so that people can read them more easily and the recording of the texts. At present the entire collection of wood-blocks at Haein-sa Temple (see p. 159) is being put onto CDs and there is a plan for translation into English in the future. In the area of education, many temples now have kindergartens or other schools attached to them. This is interesting because traditionally, in most Buddhist countries, young children learned to read and write from monks. One Buddhist University, Dongguk, has campuses in Seoul and Kyongju and there is a special university for monks and nuns called Sangha University.

Youth movements are greatly increasing. There are youth groups in schools and universities engaged in many special activities such as studying texts, traveling to different temples, reviving traditional folk dancing, and doing social work.

MONASTIC LIFE

MONASTIC LIFE

Going Forth

Background

After the Buddha Sakyamuni attained enlightenment in northern India, at first men and later women, attracted by his teaching, decided to follow him. They left their homes and joined the order that thus grew up around the Buddha. This was called "the going forth" from home to homelessness; it is still considered the first ordination ceremony in all Buddhist countries. The men and women who chose this way of life accepted to try to live according to ten training precepts as they continue to do today:

Wooden gong (Mok-Tak)

1) not to kill anything;
2) not to take anything that is not given;
3) to be celibate;
4) not to lie; 5) not to take intoxicants;
6) not to eat outside of mealtimes;
7) not to use adornments;
8) not to delight in singing, dancing or shows;
9) not to seek comfort;
10) not to amass wealth.

Soon another, more formal ordination ceremony was instigated; now, this is considered as the second ordination ceremony in all Buddhist countries. This ceremony consists of the acceptance of trying to live according to more training rules. These rules - recorded in the first part of the Buddhist texts, the Vinaya - initially came into being as solutions to problems which arose as the community lived together and grew at the time of the Buddha. Little by little rules were created according to circumstances. The men and women who received this second ordination became known as "bhikkus" and "bhikkunis" respectively.

In order to support themselves, the bhikkus and bhikkunis went on a daily alms round, gratefully receiving whatever they were given to help them on their spiritual quest. "Bhikku" means "a person who receives a share," they received a portion of the common wealth.

After the Buddha's death, the bhikkus and bhikkunis traveled and as they did, Buddhism spread. People were attracted to the Buddhist teachings of peace and tolerance and temples were built all over India, Sri Lanka, China and, eventually, most of Asia. A monk brought Buddhism to Korea and started an unbroken tradition of ordained men and women which continues up to the present day.

Let us now consider the life of bhikkus and bhikkunis in Korea. (Throughout this description, "monk" and "he" refers to men and women: their respective life-styles in Korea are identical.)

A monk brought Buddhism to Korea and started an unbroken tradition of ordained men and women which continues up to the present day.

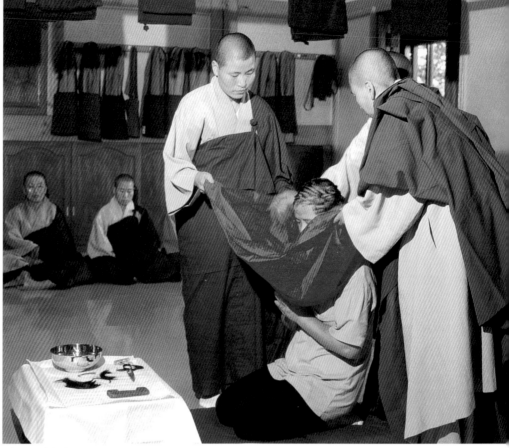

Shaving one's hair

Renunciation and Study

Anyone in Korea who wishes to be ordained in the main Buddhist monastic order, Chogye, should have completed high school and be normally healthy in order to endure the rigors of the training. Usually a man or a woman wishes to ordain in order to attain enlightenment and to help living beings. The method used to accomplish this work is careful training and ardent practice for as long as possible - even the whole life. Communal living, meditation, religious practice, the study of texts and listening to the words of great monks and nuns all form part of this way of life.

At first, the candidate becomes an aspirant. On entering the monastery, he cuts off relations with the outside world for a time, symbolized by shaving hair and beard and wearing gray or brown clothes. (Women do not shave their heads at first: this being a trial period, they would have difficulty returning home, if they so chose.) Traditionally, shaving the hair is a renunciation of rank, as well as a way to reduce vanity and to be more hygienic. During this period, the aspirant learns chanting, does chores about the

On entering the monastery, he cuts off relations with the outside world for a time, symbolized by shaving hair and beard and wearing gray or brown clothes.

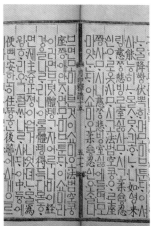
Sukbosangjul

These blocks are truly marvelous because of the evenness of the carving and the fact that there is not a single mistake in the whole collection.

monastery and cares for the senior monks. In addition, and probably most importantly, he must learn what the Buddha taught and the spiritual path ahead. For this he relies on the ancient texts as well as the commentaries written by practitioners through the ages.

Books have always been of central importance to Buddhism. Intrinsic to Buddhist philosophy is the fact that each person must study and test the teaching for himself. In all Buddhist countries, people have always been literate and the books as freely available as possible. In fact, books started with Buddhism.

Books, Binding & Printing

Most of us buy paper back books these days. Piled at airports and in book shops, they look just exactly what they are: mass produced. Obviously they pop out of a machine ready-made and that is exactly how we treat them: with no respect. We carry them around in a pocket or a bag and the covers get bent and messy but we don't really care because that is what they are meant for. No-one seems to care, even the editing is lousy!

It wasn't always like that. We used to carefully bind books, covering them in leather, embossing them with gold and silver and there were even covers made of ivory and beautiful wood. In the west, the library of a great house was very important and a special place for delving into life's secrets. The books were treasures and even today, to be left a library in someone's will is a wonderful thing.

Books started with Buddhism. One of the most important practices in Buddhism since ancient times is studying the texts and therefore they had to be available to everyone. In Sri Lanka, the texts were written down on palm leaves (specially dried, the letters were scratched into the leaf with a needle and powdered ink rubbed into the marks) in about 80 BCE. The leaves were strung together and the resulting book was preserved between two slabs of beautifully decorated, often bejewelled, wood. The result could be carried around easily and, as it

was often in the local script, everyone could read it. In China, the texts were carved on strips of bamboo, silk, stone and on wood but there seems to have been a tendency of preserving the texts in one place rather than spreading them around.

It was in Korea that printing really developed. The first example of a printed "book" in the world is a Buddhist text consisting of 12 separate sheets from separate wood-blocks, stuck together to form a scroll dating from between 706 and 751. Today, now a World Heritage treasure, the over 80,000 wood-blocks completed in 1251 of the entire collection of Buddhist texts can be seen at Haein-sa Temple, near Taegu. These blocks are truly marvelous because of the evenness of the carving and the fact that there is not a single mistake in the whole collection – unlike the paper backs of today!

In order to make copies of wood-blocks, ink is spread on the surface so that it soaks in for a few hours and then a new layer of ink is applied, a piece of mulberry paper is smoothed on top, the surface is carefully brushed with a ball of human hair (to remove any wrinkles and see that the letters are well formed on the paper) and then it is carefully peeled off and set to dry.

Due to the need to study so emphasized in Buddhism, books were in heavy demand. The labor intensive method of printing from the wood blocks was time consuming and costly. So a more available method had to be sought out: someone had to invent moveable type. And this is what happened. The characters were cast in the same way as coins and then lined up to print texts. The first book to be printed was The Selected Teachings of Buddhist Sages and Son Masters in 1377 – long before Gutenberg in the middle of the fifteenth century!!!

From single sheets, to many stuck together in a scroll or in a screen, to printed sheets, the evolution of the book has played a central role in the development of culture. Once moveable type was invented, then the printed sheets had to be fixed together and protected. This is where the creation of book covers came into being and more efficient binding techniques were used.

Books were always prized and loved. In order to express and underline this feeling, beautiful covers were created. In Korea, embossed mulberry paper was usually used. The embossing formed a back-drop pattern and the covers were

The first book to be printed was The Selected Teachings of Buddhist Sages and Son Masters in 1377 - long before Gutenberg in the middle of the fifteenth century!!!

often dyed and sometimes oiled. The designs used were mostly traditional ones like water chestnuts, one of the most popular because, as the plant grows near the edge of ponds, people regarded it as a good luck charm for preventing the burning down of their homes – and of the books. Also popular was the swastika, a symbol of peace and good luck in Asia. Lotuses, thunder clouds, tortoise shell and bats – the Korean name is similar to the word for good luck – were common motifs.

Binding was traditionally done with cord. The whole book was put together with a strand running length-wise on the back and on the front and then four horizontal strands held the pages together. Of course the technique was specialized and required dexterity and experience to execute well.

Alas, all of this is long past and only available at great expense today. So, as paper backs are the current book form, maybe we have to learn to love them and treat them more decently!

After about one year, it is then decided whether or not the candidate is suitable for monastic life and, if so, he chooses a teacher – or they choose each other.

The aspirant is given ordination and takes the first set of basic training rules: the ten precepts which constitute the "going forth." The teacher takes care of the disciple, now called a sami, (samini for women), materially and spiritually. The disciple, in turn, serves his teacher.

Next the young monk is sent to one of the Monks' Colleges. These are special institutions where the sami (or samini, separately) study the texts more deeply, learn Chinese characters, chanting and all the other talents required for a fully ordained member of the Buddhist community. In addition, these days there is a large number of more modern subjects available. Examples include English, psychology, techniques for teaching the young and the old are included in the curriculum. The most important lessons are in the art of communal living. As all the members of one year will stay together in one large room for the four years, they must learn to live harmoniously.

The young monk is sent to one of the Monks' Colleges. These are special institutions where the sami (or samini, separately) study the texts more deeply, learn Chinese characters, chanting and all the other talents required for a fully ordained member of the Buddhist community.

Ordination

Full Ordination

After five years, if the teacher sees fit, the novice is sent for the second ordination and becomes a bhikkhu (bhikkhuni for women) or a full member of the monastic community or Sangha. This ceremony is preceded by five days of extra training and lectures.

Daily Life

Morning

Pray that the whole universe will hear this sound and may all painful places be brightened.

The day begins at 3 a.m. One monk rises a little earlier, washes, and puts on his ceremonial robes. Slowly, he walks to each part of the monastery beating a mokt'ak (a hollowed, wooden, bell-shaped percussion instrument) and chanting as he goes. The clear sound of the mokt'ak breaks the stillness of the pre-dawn hours...

"Pray that the whole universe will hear this sound and may all painful places be brightened. May the hells, ghosts and animals be relieved of suffering, and may all problems disappear so that all living beings may properly awake."

This wake-up ceremony is carried out every day of every year regardless of the weather. On hearing the mokt'ak,

Morning

The Drum   The Song

The Wooden Fish   The huge bell

the monks get up, fold and put away their bedding, and wash (they sleep in their clothes). In the countryside, traditionally, they often wash in a stream or from a large stone bowl where water collects. After a short time, the large bell, followed by the drum, gong and wooden fish, are sounded and all monks go to the Main Hall for chanting.

The large bell, drum, gong and wooden fish each represent a section of the world of living beings. The large bell calls those who have become decadent. The drum, made of an animal skin, calls the animals; and the cloud-shaped gong calls the beings of the air. The log carved into the shape of a fish calls all that live in water. Every living thing is called to listen to the chanting of the words of liberation taught by the Buddha and to follow that wisdom, if they so wish.

After communal chanting, each monk returns to his place. The students go to the study hall; the meditating monks go to the meditation hall (in the meditation seasons they merely bow in the meditation hall and sit); and the working monks go to their place of duty. At about 6 a.m., breakfast takes place.

Breakfast traditionally consists of rice porridge and pickles which the community eats together in silence in a formal style from a set of four individual bowls. A spoon is used along with chopsticks, a custom which is unique to Korea.

Spoons & Chopsticks:
History, Culture and Etiquette

Koreans are the only far easterners to use spoons to eat both rice and soup regularly. The Chinese have those chinaware spoons for soup but eat the rest with chopsticks only. Koreans use spoons all the time; two theories prevail about this practice. Eighty percent of Korean food consists of soups, often served in a communal pot in which everyone dips. Also Koreans love to put rice into the soup and eat the two together: impossible to eat with chopsticks. Another plausible reason lies in the habit of mixing rice with other grains making the whole rather non-sticky and therefore difficult to carry to the mouth with chopsticks

Every living thing is called to listen to the chanting of the words of liberation taught by the Buddha and to follow that wisdom, if they so wish.

Wooden Fish(Mok-Eo)

As far as chopsticks are concerned, it is claimed that Korean chopsticks are the easiest and most convenient to use. Japanese hopsticks are too thin and Chinese chopsticks are hardly shaped at all.

because the mass lacks in adhesiveness. This is particularly true in the case of adding barley and millet which were and are wide spread customs. In fact in hard times, rice became a luxury to Koreans and they subsisted mostly on barley - no stick there!

Whatever the reason, bronze spoons and chopsticks have been unearthed from the royal tomb of King Munyong of Paekje (r. 501-523), among other places, which are very similar to those found in China making it highly likely that either Koreans copied Chinese spoons or they used imported ones. But the Chinese stopped using spoons on a regular basis and Koreans continued.

Other spoons, dating from the Unified Shilla Period (668 - 932) were excavated. These show straighter handles and are not found in China. Those dating after the eighth century were absolutely unlike any Chinese ones. As a similar style is found in Japan, it is surmised that Korea exported them to that country. Members of the royal court had to use silver chopsticks and spoon because poison discolors silver, warning the user. Women of the court had a silver spoon which accompanied their personal dagger which they always carried so that it was ever available. The dagger was small with a very sharp blade just long enough to reach the heart, ready for suicide in order to avoid being raped in times of invasion.

Ancient spoons and chopsticks were made of copper, brass or silver. From the Koryo Period (932-1392), the spoons had curved handles which looked like a swallow's tail. Sometimes the handle ended in a knot. The spoon was also quite long and not very wide. It was not until the early Choson Period (1392-1910) that the spoons became flatter and wider and shaped like a lotus petal. After the middle of the Choson Period, the handles became longer and thicker and straighter and the round part became very round.

As far as chopsticks are concerned, it is claimed that Korean chopsticks are the easiest and most convenient to use. Japanese hopsticks are too thin and Chinese chopsticks are hardly shaped at all. Many a foreign visitor would dispute this claim when faced with the highly slippery prospect of eating with the common metal Korean chopstick!

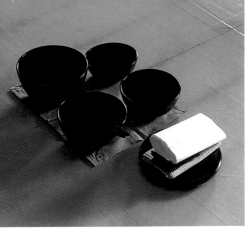

Bowls

Even though history is not of the greatest interest, it is extraordinary to think that such mundane things as eating implements carry history, geography, art and technology all wrapped up in them. In addition, there is a tremendous amount of culture and etiquette contained in the lowly spoon.

Customs concerning spoons are very strict. When setting the table each place is set with rice, soup, spoon and chopsticks. Rice comes first, then the soup followed by the spoon and then the chopsticks. (Is this in order of importance? In which case is the spoon more important than the chopsticks?) As far as table etiquette is concerned, Koreans never put the spoon down on the table until they have finished eating. When laying it to rest during the meal, the spoon is placed on the side of the rice bowl or in the soup bowl. The chopsticks can be placed on the table when the eater is occupied with other aspects of the meal but never the spoon. Also a spoon held too high up the handle foretells a marriage far from home. And anyone holding the spoon too far down the handle is simply uncouth — and might have to suffer dirty fingers.

When laying it to rest during the meal, the spoon is placed on the side of the rice bowl or in the soup bowl.

If you really want to change your fortune, here's how. You go to a fortune teller who decides on a more lucky or more auspicious name and has it engraved on your spoon. You then proceed to only use that spoon for a long time (one year?) and the new, luckier name changes everything for you. At least that is what a friend of mine did. I'm sorry to report that, as I lost sight of the person, I don't know the outcome so let's just believe the fortune teller and expect the best of all possibilities.

Traditionally newly weds prepare the spoons and chopsticks (and other things) which they will use until their death. The sumptuous 100 day celebration of a baby (feted because it has lived through the many perils of early infancy) is when the child receives his first set of spoon and chopsticks.

After breakfast is the most important part of the day because the air and minds of the monks are clear. Activities continue with the studying monks often receiving their main instruction at this time.

Midday

Chanting and offering rice, thus remembering the Buddha's custom of eating once a day, take place at 10:30 a.m. After the ceremony, the monks have lunch. They chant before and during the meal and remind themselves to take food to sustain the body, not from greed or from a desire to beautify themselves.

"Let us reflect upon the human efforts that have made this meal possible, and ask ourselves whether we deserve this offering. Let us rid ourselves of greed and regard this meal as medicine to help us to see the truth and to reach the great wisdom beyond."

Lunch is the main meal of the day for the Buddha did not eat in the evening. In China, due to climatic changes - being often much colder than India - this was changed. However, if the monks do eat, the food is taken in the spirit of medicine. (Traditionally, in Korea, as monks did not eat in the evening, they merely rubbed their grumbling bellies with a stone. Thus evening food is referred to as "medicine rock," in Korean.)

A meal using the traditional four bowls

Afternoon and Evening

After lunch and a short free period, all return to their respective activities until supper-time at about 5 p.m. (depending on the season—it is earlier in the winter than in the summer). An hour or so later, the sound of the big temple bell announces chanting:

"May all living things who hear this bell be relieved from suffering, develop wisdom and attain enlightenment. May we all live in peace..."

Quiet study or meditation follows. Then at about 10 p.m. the beds are rolled out and the lights switched off.

Meditation Life

Meditation is very much stressed in Korean Buddhism and many monks and nuns spend their whole life in meditation.

Meditation is very much stressed in Korean Buddhism and many monks and nuns spend their whole life in meditation. In all Buddhist schools in all countries, meditation is considered the main means for attaining enlightenment. The year is divided into meditation seasons, winter and summer, and free seasons, spring and autumn. The winter retreat begins on the 15th of the 10th lunar month and continues until the 15th of the 1st lunar month (roughly November to February). The summer season starts on the 15th of the 4th lunar month and ends on the 15th of the 7th lunar month (roughly May to August).

About two weeks before the season begins, monks and nuns start to look for a meditation hall where they can spend the season. Once the season starts, they are not permitted to leave the monastery until it is over.

To eliminate distractions, there is neither chanting, nor reading and even talking about the Buddha is discouraged. All potential obstructions to concentration are eliminated to permit the meditator to make the breakthrough to enlightenment. Many monks observe silence and others may give up reclining for a certain period.

There are four meditation sessions a day: pre-dawn, morning, afternoon and evening. Silent meals are taken with the rest of the residential community.

Meditation

Bowls and robes

Before a session starts, a hollowed-out bamboo rod ("chuk-bi" in Korean) is struck three times. Fifty minutes later, the chuk-bi is sounded once only before the ten minute walking meditation period. Then all sit down again to continue the sitting meditation. At the end of the session, the chuk-bi is again struck three times.

Once a year, in many temples–twice in the bigger ones– there is an intensive, one-week period. At that time, the meditators practice up to twenty hours a day and do not recline. After this, many continue the exercise and occasionally even extend it to years!

Traditionally, meditating monks have few possessions and what they have can be packed into a backpack together with their bowls for eating and robes for chanting. In the search for enlightenment, meditating monks are unattached as clouds in the sky, or as flowing mountain streams. Some remain in the same temple for three or five years, others move about. Some only meditate for a short while, others for the whole life. Once enlightenment is attained, the monk has a duty to teach others.

The Year

Each year is naturally divided into four seasons. Temple life, ever as close to nature as possible, follows the seasons and Korea's climate has a sharp distinction between the very cold, dry winter, the balmy spring and autumn and the humid, sweltering summer. Thus the summer and winter are reserved for meditation and retreat, and the spring and autumn for wandering, seeking instruction and doing service.

The ordained members of the Sangha have their own distinctive robes. Based on traditional Korean clothes, the season are well accommodated.

Clothes to Suit the Climate

Some say that each color has a meaning, at least that is what I've been told. This results in certain customs. In India the young bride-to-be is dressed in red and in Korea the young bride on her traditional honeymoon wears a crimson coat. Red is considered the color of passion. In the

> Traditionally,
> meditating monks
> have few
> possessions and
> what they have
> can be packed into
> a backpack
> together with their
> bowls for eating
> and robes for
> chanting.

Bamboo rod
(Chuk-bi)

western world, the bride-to-be wears white, the color of purity. Buddhist monks in Sri Lanka wear saffron (yellow) because it is the color of intelligence. Originally the wandering philosophers (sadhus) of ancient India wore gherva, a reddish color derived from rubbing bricks on white cloth. This signified the five elements - earth, water, fire, air and ether - and the fact that the person had passed out of society, passed out of the established norms and duties of human life in an effort to gain wisdom and understanding.

When Buddhism passed to China in about 1st century CE, the Chinese changed the yellow, of which they are not so fond, to grey and so in Korea, ordained Buddhists (and lay people doing special practice) wear grey. The color of ashes - recalling Buddhists' customary future cremation - and all colors mixed, grey comes in many shades from light to almost black. The cloth used for the robes is in varying thicknesses and textures of fabric in order to be suitable for the rigorous extremes of the Korean climate.

Traditionally the clothes were made of the cheapest and most readily available cloth. Special kinds of hand woven cotton (which were not so special way back when) suitable for the very distinct seasons of spring, autumn and winter were used and ramie or linen were considered best for the summer. As the clothes were large, many layers could be heaped on below the outer grey wear. Therefore, even though the fabrics used were of varying thicknesses, compensation for the basic lack of warmth of cotton could be acquired by heaping up layers below.

Basic monks' clothes consist of an array of garments. Based on the traditional Korean hanbok, monks' clothes are made one "ch'i" larger everywhere (a ch'i is a traditional measurement which equals the width of the base of the first finger.) The clothes consist of very baggy pants, bhaji; a short working jacket, choksam; a longer formal jacket with a flowing tie in front, dongbanga; and an overcoat, drumagi. In addition, there is the ceremonial dress. The main robe is called a changsam and as it is made of 10 meters of cloth, it is very large and flowing, reaching down to the ankles and has pleats in the skirt part. Over this is worn the Buddhist robe, a garment made of patches of brown cloth and secured to the left with a Turk's Head knot, leaving the right shoulder uncovered - sign of respect in ancient India. It is made of patches because it therefore has no commercial value and some say that it is an image of the paddy fields through which the Buddha spent many years wandering...

Let us take a look at the clothes in more detail. There are the pants, bhaji in Korean, which are very baggy and comfortable. The fabric is gathered at the waist with a belt which is tied at the side. At the ankle, the bagginess is gathered and folded using another piece of cloth to tie it, traditionally, or elastic, these days. Then there is the working jacket, choksam. It is short, with short sleeves, large pockets in the front and it is done up with buttons or press fasteners. If you are going out of the temple, you put a coat, drumagi, on top of this. The coat is long and flowing and it is secured with a tie on the inner left and a long flowing tie on the outer right. The sleeves are long and it usually has no pockets, just two holes through which you can put your hands to adjust the inner garments! If you are receiving guests in the temple, you wear a dongbanga. This is a short jacket - longer than the working one — which has a tie in the front like the coat and deep pockets inside.

Probably the most interesting types of monks' clothes are the summer, heavily starched ramie and linen, and the wonderful padded winter fare.

Korean summers are hot (35 degrees Centigrade) and humid (85%-95%). Ramie and linen are not only porous allowing the skin to breathe but when starched, the clothes stand out from the body. Everyone always wants to touch the cloth because it looks so rough and coarse, but I can assure you, there is nothing so comfortable for the climate! Unfortunately, these clothes used to be cheap but are now terribly expensive...

Korean winters are cold, the temperature often going down to -10 or -20 degrees Centigrade. Although layers can and are worn under the loose clothes, this is not enough. You need a barrier against the wind and the dry cold. Originally introduced from China, cotton-wool padded clothes, nubi in Korean, are worn.

To make nubi clothes requires an enormous amount of time. However, once made, if they are well cared for, they last a long time. (While writing this, I am wearing a nubi joki, vest or waistcoat, which is at least 15 years old!) First

> If you are going out of the temple, you put a coat, drumagi, on top of this. The coat is long and flowing and it is secured with a tie on the inner left and a long flowing tie on the outer right. The sleeves are long and it usually has no pockets, just two holes through which you can put your hands to adjust the inner garments!

of all the clothes are cut out and then, traditionally, straight parallel lines are ironed on with an indo, a small cast-iron, iron which is thrust into hot oak embers, wiped off on a piece of cloth and used to make the lines to be stitched through the layers to keep the cotton wool in place. This piece of cloth is placed on top of a layer of cotton wool which has been placed on top of another layer of cloth. The lines are stitched in perfectly even stitches using waxed thread. (Some people hold a candle below to catch the needle when it is pulled through so that it doesn't go into the fingers.) Before this kind of nubi, Koreans used to stitch around the edge only. Then, when the garment was dirty, it was unstitched, the cloth washed, boiled and starched and then it was all sewed up again! Needless to say, these days, not many people have time to unsew and sew up clothes all the time. Therefore nubi clothes are popular.

Although the ordained Sangha's robes are rather interesting to the visitor, they are very practical and comfortable to wear. The bagginess means that they last a long time and life on the floor (continual getting up and down, sitting cross-legged) is easy. Don't ever try these clothes yourself because you may find them so convenient that you never want to take them off!

At different times during the year, there are changes in schedule. When more manpower is required for agricultural activities, all join in. In the early spring there is a special week for lay people. During that week, the monks look after the lay people, who are doing special religious practices, and do some extra practice themselves. Bowing, reading texts, reciting sacred words and so on are all part of the way people practice Buddhism and try to improve themselves.

Later Life

Once training is completed, monks chose from different ways of life. Some monks go to university; some are called upon (especially as they get older) to do administrative jobs. Sometimes a group will decide to do a three-year long meditation retreat; sometimes monks will go abroad to teach. Often, they will change, too. A teaching monk, for example, may return to meditation for a time.

> **Sometimes a group will decide to do a three-year long meditation retreat; sometimes monks will go abroad to teach. Often, they will change, too. A teaching monk, for example, may return to meditation for a time.**

Many monks and nuns specialize in a particular activity. There are famous artists, there are professors, doctors, a dentist and so on. One of the most popular "professions" to chose is calligraphy. Because of the heavy reliance on Chinese characters and the traditional respect given to the learned and artistic, a calligrapher is a special person in Korean society. Below we have used the Confucian gentleman as our subject. Today, although there are a lot of monks who do calligraphy, there are still many laypeople as well. (In fact, if you should visit a class, you'd be surprised at the number of people who plan their life around calligraphy!) Let us take a look at:

The Four Friends: Brushes and Loyalty

Every self-respecting Korean (Confucian) gentleman had four friends: his brush, his ink stick, his ink stone, and his paper: constant, loyal and a source of joy. These four things were always available in the gentleman's room and whenever he was bored, it was to their friendship that he turned.

What is a friend? Someone you can rely on, someone you can turn to, someone who is constant, unchanging in loyalty, whose company you enjoy. Well, every self-respecting Korean (Confucian) gentleman had four friends: his brush, his ink stick, his ink stone, and his paper: constant, loyal and a source of joy. These four things were always available in the gentleman's room and whenever he was bored, it was to their friendship that he turned.

We tried to find a finer analogy between the Four Friends and the life values that they might represent which could have been handed down through the long generations of the rich cultural heritage of Korean humor, but failed. So it seems to be up to us to invent something! The brush you can imagine easily. It represents steadfastness, companionship. It accompanied that self-respecting gentleman everywhere because in those days there were no places to rush to and everyone wasn't "busy." In fact non-busyness was the order of the day. In spite of this hard adherence to doing nothing, boredom hit every now again and so, according to the National Treasure of brushes, Mr. Kwong Jin-tae, the gentleman would take up his trusty brush and paint a picture - to relieve the boredom. In order to create the art work, he needed an ink stick and an ink stone which represent constancy, loyalty, and paper, the fourth of the Four Friends, which represents enjoyment because it comes in many different forms.

It seemed a good idea to begin with the brush because it was the most constant friend. In order to learn about brushes, we turned to the maestro, Mr. Kwong Jin-tae, who is the National Living Treasure of Brushes. It was a joy to meet him. The story of his life consists of brushes and almost nothing else. He started making them when he was 14 years-old; of course I asked why. "Well," He replied, "a man visited our house and, because we were so poor and I had no other idea, I thought it was a good choice." He learnt with his teacher for ten years and then set out on his own. His big break came after the Korean war, when everything was destroyed: the first thing that everyone wanted and needed was a brush. "There were only 28 brush makers in Korea at the time, so we all did a roaring business!" He continued, " You have to remember that in those days the brush was everything. Starting from the carpenter who marked the place where he was going to cut the wood, brushes were central to every aspect of life. After all there were no pens and no pencils then. In the past, men didn't rush around attending power luncheons or doing international deals. They carried their brush in the sleeve of their coat (rolled up in a little rice stalk mat to keep it straight) and went around to contests, or joined friends to write poetry."

"Can you do calligraphy?" I asked Mr. Kwong. "Oh no," he replied, " I only know how to make brushes. In fact for most of my life I get up in the morning, eatsomething and then just make brushes until midnight." "Yes" said his wife, "We've been married for 43 years and all we've done is make brushes." Sounded like a complaint so I checked "Are you bored?" "Oh no! There's no time to be bored, we just make brushes." Her husband quickly explained, "In those days there was no TV, no radio and we didn't know what was going on in the world at all, we just made brushes."

Brushes in Korea have a sketchily known history, like many things Korean, either there were no records kept or they were destroyed. Apart from a brush found in a tomb dating back 2,000 years, little is known about brushes beyond about 500 years back. There were 200 kinds of brushes when Mr Kwong started. Brushes were not only used for marking something (carpenters) and writing, but

There were 200 kinds of brushes when Mr Kwong started. Brushes were not only used for marking something (carpenters) and writing, but they played an important role in cloth making and designing, and many household jobs. Nowadays, Mr. Kwong only makes calligraphy brushes.

Brushes

Brush-making is difficult, it's a craft, you can't be greedy, you can't be interested in money if you really want to do it.

they played an important role in cloth making and designing, and many household jobs. Nowadays, Mr. Kwong only makes calligraphy brushes.

By this time I was really curious, I hadn't expected brushes to be so interesting. "So what are brushes made of?" I finally asked. "The best brushes are made of the hair of a big male goat. The hair should be smooth, strong and straight and so the best hair is cut after snow falls of January and February. The absolute best is the hair of the white goats from Northern Cholla Province by the sea and the hair from under the legs is really fine because it has been protected. Live goats are not shorn, the hair is removed from dead animals." In addition to goat's hair, a baby's first hair makes an excellent brush – Mr. Kwong's personal favorite. Feathers can be used and sometimes small brushes can be made from squirrel tail hair. Unusual brushes are made of bamboo finely shredded with a needle (must take forever) and tightly bound pine needles.

Once you have the goat hair, it has to be treated in order to remove the natural oil in it – otherwise it won't hold the ink. The hair is laid down with layers of ash and a heavy, flat weight is placed on top in order to squeeze out the oil. This is the traditional method, nowadays they use an electrically heated iron block which squeezes the oil – with the ash – in just five minutes. Then the bristles are put together and tied with string. For the king or famous scholars, gold and silver thread was used. The end which is to be fitted into the handle is burned to make the base more solid. Mr. Kwong showed us that the properly made base cannot be squeezed. After that, the bound bristles are fitted into the handle.

Brush handles are made of almost anything: china, silver, iron, brass, horn, and bamboo. Mr. Kwong prefers bamboo but his son complains that in the shop sometimes the bamboo warps and no-one wants to buy the brush. There are no rules as to the length of the handle, it should just look and feel nice. When not in use, brushes are stored hanging on special stands made of wood. In this way they dry and don't rot.

Finally, I asked Mr. Kwong about how to judge a good brush. "It should be very soft, should look nice, be even pretty. And when you squeeze the bristles together, the

Traditionally ink came in sticks, very small ones long ago. Pine wood was burnt and the soot collected. This was then mixed with pine resin, formed into rectangular sticks and dried. As it was a precious substance, it was decorated with special, auspicious Chinese characters which were engraved on the stick.

Inksticks

tip makes a very slight curve, it isn't straight."

I looked around the apartment as we were leaving. "So, how many apprentices do you have to carry on?" He bowed his head, "No-one is interested these days. They all want to go and learn driving. Brush-making is difficult, it's a craft, you can't be greedy, you can't be interested in money if you really want to do it." "And your son?" I asked brightly. "Oh, he learnt in the womb, of course," Mr. Kwong's wife said, "he knows how to make brushes." "But he never does..." Mr Kwong interjected.

Ink, Ink-stones and Constancy

Every self-respecting Confucian gentlemen had Four Friends, four constant companions to his life. These things, brush, ink stick, ink stone and paper, provided him with enjoyment as well as the constancy and loyalty you would expect of a friend. Let us now take a look at the ink and the stones that it was ground on.

Traditionally ink came in sticks, very small ones long ago. Pine wood was burnt and the soot collected. This was then mixed with pine resin, formed into rectangular sticks and dried. As it was a precious substance, it was decorated with special, auspicious Chinese characters which were engraved on the stick. Sometimes the characters were painted another color, or gold and silver was applied. Nowadays, when everything has to be in such huge quantities due to the enormous population of the world, carbon is used and it is mixed with different substances to produce rather larger sticks which are decorated in the same fashion and even, sometimes, perfumed.

Now the aforementioned gentleman had a problem if he was in a hurry to relieve his boredom. In order to have the ink to paint the picture, he had to spend a number of hours rubbing the ink stick on the fine surface of the ink stone with a little water to create the right consistency of ink for his amusement. It is just possible that his ink stone was of superior quality and had a tightly fitting cover. If so, then the ink of the last time had not dried up but if not, he had to make new ink. He had to rub the ink stick in rhythmic, circle motions on his fine ink stone, adding a drop of water

Inkstone

every now and again until he had the ink he needed. (Machines are used today, of course.)

Usually ink stones are made of a black stone which is relatively soft to carve. Elaborately decorated on the top, they vary enormously from the smallest which can be about the size of a finger, to the biggest, about the size of a roof tile. The usual design is one in which there is an elevated area and a slope with a smaller area in which the ink can collect as you grind away. The edges are raised and the grain of the stone is very fine.

Additional, non-essential tools accompanied the gentleman. A water dropper, a ceramic or porcelain closed jug which had a small hole so that the quantity of water can be regulated. (These water droppers are now collectors' items because they come in many different sizes and shapes and are often made of fine ceramic, beautifully gazed and decorated.) A useful tool is a very interesting holder made of bamboo with small, two-ended, bamboo buttons to lock the ink stick into place. The hands remain clean and even a very used, thus short, ink stick can be ground to the end. There is one more "appliance" in the ensemble: an ink pot. This is a lovely round or oval ceramic object, often exquisitely painted, with a top and bottom of the same size. Ink can be kept from drying out in it. Back to the ink stones...

Ink stones are made in various shapes and with various designs. Usually rectangular, some stones are round, oval, square, hexagonal or octagonal and occasionally they come in no particular shape or in the form of the design which has been carved on the back. The expensive variety are actually carved, the cheaper ones are made from the powder of the stone, reconstituted with a binding substance and pressed into a mold.

The carvings on the lid of the ink stone are, of course, highly symbolic. Most popular are the classic ten symbols of longevity; one or more are combined to form the decoration. These are: the sun, clouds, water, rocks, tortoises, cranes, deer, pines, bamboo and pullch' o, the fungus of immortality. Other favorites come from the group known as the "four gentlemen" (noble symbols): bamboo, pine, chrysanthemums and orchids. Sometimes there is a dragon, a crane, a turtle, a phoenix, grapes, plum blossom, an elixir bottle, a persimmon, a fish, or Chinese characters. As far as the shops seen these days, tortoises seem to be the front runners in popularity for decorating an inkstone.

And so the Confucian gentleman passed his days grinding his ink stick on his ink stone, smoothing out the paper to cover with lovely strokes from his brush — and he didn't die of stress-related diseases.

Chamber Pots, Hats and Vases

You may wonder what on earth chamber pots, hats and vases could possibly have in common. In most places, nothing, it is true. But in Korea, they are (let's make it were) all made of paper, yes paper. In Korea, paper was not only essential, it was involved in every aspect of life... and still is.

Traditionally in summer, the elegant Confucian gentleman sat in his wooden floored room with the windows/doors hitched up so that the air could circulate freely and create a lovely soft, cool breeze. Dressed in white, flowing, finest ramie clothes, his hair carefully knotted under his horse-hair hat, he would sit on an intricately woven mat or cushion and, drawing his lovely little wooden desk to him, he set to occupying his time with his Four Friends: his brush, ink stick, ink stone and paper.

After grinding the ink stick with occasional drops of water on the ink stone, he would smooth out a piece of fine, fresh paper on his desk, carefully placing special long weights at the top and the bottom. Then, dipping his brush into the ink, he would write a few lines of poetry in energetic, emotional strokes. The Four Friends had once more proved loyal, constant and a source of enjoyment.

The paper will have been chosen from among thousands of different inds. Korean paper is made of mulberry pulp mixed with what is called "pulp" — which is recycled paper. There is no right/best/good paper for any given thing, everything depends on your personal taste. "Some prefer smoother paper, some prefer more absorbent paper, some prefer more pliable paper; it all depends on the individual taste. Generally though, good calligraphers like

There is no right/best/good paper for any given thing, everything depends on your personal taste. "Some prefer smoother paper, some prefer more absorbent paper, some prefer more pliable paper; it all depends on the individual taste.

Paper

Large sheets of pulp-rich paper were stuck together in layers and then dipped in vats of soya bean oil. The result was a very strong, thick paper which was laid down on the floor in squares with the edges overlapping, stuck down with glue.

very absorbent paper," said my interviewee, Chi-kwang Sunim. An ordained Buddhist in Korea for nearly 20 years, one of her constant interests has been paper. "You can't imagine the variety! When we were making paper during a special workshop recently, we chopped up grass, pine needles, flowers, almost anything to create a different texture, a different smell, a different color of paper. (Actually, I had never really thought much about paper, just used it. As the world of variety and possible uses opened up before my eyes, I became quite engrossed! I imagined rose paper, lily paper, lilac paper and so on...) Then we used only natural materials so the paper would be stronger, last longer and stay the same color, not fading or discoloring with age."

Chi-kwang went on to explain that natural bleaches really make a difference. I knew normal bleach, chlorine water, but didn't know anything about natural bleaches, and so I asked. "Oh, the stalks of different plants like rice or better still buckwheat are burnt and the pulp is boiled with the ash. This produces a really marvelous paper."

I began to wonder just how far paper could go. And then I was told. "There are paper umbrellas, raincoats, vases, boxes, floor panels, chamber pots and even shoes." (Shoes of cardboard, yes. But paper shoes?) The soles, I was soon told, are made of layers of paper stuck together with glue and the rest of the shoe is made of woven paper, the basis of many traditional household articles - all carefully varnished, or more traditionally oiled - stitched together with paper string.

Paper is cut into long strips and then rolled into long worm-like pieces. It is these that are woven. Rather naively I began to wonder about the practicality of walking in the rain in a paper raincoat with my paper umbrella in my paper shoes! "All are woven from these worm-like pieces of paper string and treated. The umbrella and shoes are varnished with lacquer and the raincoat is treated with wild sesame oil. They're very strong, you know," Chi-kwang assured me.

Cushion covers, table and floor mats, book covers, and vases are all made of woven paper. Vases are carefully lacquered on the inside to make them able to hold water. And then there is the traditional Korean floor covering - before linoleum.

Offerings of food are placed on an altar and monks chant, accompanied by the periodic ringing of small hand bells and the rhythmic beating of the mokt' ak.

Korean floors in the rooms traditionally inhabited during winter, when the temperature hovers between 0 and -20 degrees Centigrade, were heated under the floor. The floors were made of huge stones and earth under which flues conducted hot air from a fire made in the adjoining kitchen to the external chimney. The floor was covered with paper.

Large sheets of pulp-rich paper were stuck together in layers and then dipped in vats of soya bean oil. The result was a very strong, thick paper which was laid down on the floor in squares with the edges overlapping, stuck down with glue. (Of course things have changed and now fish oil is usually used.) The paper was then lacquered a number of times. These floors start life a bright yellow which mellows to a rich chestnut as time goes by. In fact, if the floor is sand-papered and lacquered again every year, the paper lasts for ever.

It is impossible to finish an article on paper without mentioning today. Long ago, clothes were made of paper and this is a new trend on the catwalk. Wedding dresses, scarves, hats and suits are all being made of paper. The best is 100% mulberry paper. The sheets are crumpled up over and over again to make the paper strong and give it a lacy look. Then the clothes are stitched and worn and even washed – though carefully.

Offerings for the Buddha

Whatever the activity, each member of the temple continues throughout his life to do his best to attain enlightenment. Living a simple life, being vegetarian, abstaining from cigarettes and alcohol, being celibate, and dedicating his actions to the welfare of all beings are ways in which Buddhist monks try to improve the world.

Buddhist Ceremonies

Apart from the three daily chanting periods, there are special ceremonies for other occasions. Memorial services are quite frequent. Offerings of food are placed on an altar and monks chant, accompanied by the periodic ringing of

Chanting in Hades Hall

small hand bells and the rhythmic beating of the mokt'ak.

Every two weeks, on the day the monks shave their heads, and wash and mend clothes; there is a ceremony and teaching delivered by a senior monk; the ceremony is open to the public. This is the time for large meetings to take place in order to discuss temple problems or changes - Buddhist temples are very democratic.

The five main Buddhist holidays are richly celebrated each year, according to the lunar calendar: the Buddha's Leaving Home (2nd month, 8th day), the Buddha's Death (2nd month, 15th day), the Buddha's Birthday, the main event of the year, (4th month, 8th day), "All Spirits' Day" (7th month, 15th day), and Enlightenment Day (12th month, 8th day). For the Buddha's Birthday, in particular, Koreans resort to a purely Korean phenomenon: the lotus lantern.

Unique to Korea: Lotus Lanterns

It's really hard to pinpoint what it is that makes a lantern so special. Faces glow in the light and there seems to be some hidden delight and gentleness in carrying a lantern. I know that this is true for Seoul, Korea, because every year there are many small local parades of lanterns to celebrate the Buddha's Birthday in May and people come in droves to see the lanterns and many more than you would expect come to carry a lantern around the neighborhood. It seems such a simple activity and yet people of all ages love it.

In Korea, lanterns are a major focus of one of the most important yearly events called Buddha's Birthday. Celebrated on the 8th day of the 4th lunar month every year, Koreans believe that that is the day the Buddha Sakyamuni was born in northeastern India. (The Buddhist year is calculated from the Buddha's death which was 2500 years ago in 1956.) The Buddha was a man who spent his life teaching anyone who was interested in trying to understand reality. He taught people how to develop from a state of ignorance into true wisdom, symbolized by lotus lanterns.Unique to Korea, lotus lanterns consist of the symbols of the lotus flower and a candle. The lotus, a common symbol in Buddhism, represents the process of shedding ignorance (darkness, growing towards the light from the mud) to attain wisdom (light, the opening of the flower in the sunlight). Making lanterns in the shape of lotuses renacts the aspiration of everyone for wisdom. The candle inside symbolizes the attainment of wisdom. The occurrence of these lanterns is first recorded in 551 in the Shilla Kingdom and their popularity reached a climax in the Koryo Dynasty when there were parades of up to 10,000 lanterns. King T'aejo (r. 918-943) mentions in his Ten Injunctions – a summing up of the founder of the Koryo Dynasty's political philosophy and religious belief – that "the hanging and parading of lotus lanterns is serving the Buddha." (Injunction No. 6 adapted.) As at Hallowe'en in the USA or Guy Fawkes in the UK, children used to carry the materials for the lantern-to-be from house to house

Every year there are many small local parades of lanterns to celebrate the Buddha's Birthday in May and people come in droves to see the lanterns and many more than you would expect come to carry a lantern around the neighborhood.

Parade of Buddha's Birthday

collecting money, candies or food.

Lotus lanterns have to be seen to be believed. The beauty of them hanging and casting a mystic light filtered through pink, vermillion, yellow or cyclamen into the dark night is breath-taking. Maybe it is the beauty, maybe it is the spellbinding atmosphere that causes people to be unable to imagine how these lanterns are made. Lotus Lantern International Buddhist Center made the biggest lotus lantern in the world which went into the 1989 Guinness Book of World Records, and therefore they consider themselves expert in the art. Here is the process.

Traditionally, the frames were made of bamboo. The strips of bamboo were molded into hexagonal shapes and the joints secured. A long thin piece of bamboo made the handle. Nowadays, wire is used and the frames come ready made. For the petals, light-weight paper was dyed, cut into the desired size of rectangles and piled in stacks of 20 or 30 pieces. Then each stack was dampened and strapped tightly to a bottle. The string securing it to the bottle was wound round and round with a little space between each turn. A piece of wooden board with a hole the size of the circum-ference of the bottle (looking a little like a toilet seat) was placed over the neck of the bottle and then pressed down with enormous power forcing the string and paper to the bottom of the bottle and creating the pleats of the petals. After a couple of minutes, the string is carefully unwound and the paper cautiously removed and set aside for drying on the warm, heated floor – Korean houses and apartments have heated floors, a traditional luxury. These days the petals come ready made, too!

Once each stack of pleated, curved paper is dry, it is

Parade of Buddha's Birthday

Festival of Lanterns

ready for separating and making into petals. Each piece of paper is gently held and the tip is twisted with a little paste to form a point.

Now, back to the frame. Over the frame, white paper is pasted. When the frame and the petals are dry, then the lantern is ready to be assembled. Paste is applied to about two or three centimeters of the base (away from the point) of the petal and then it is stuck at the upper end of the lantern with the point just going over the edge of the frame. After that the petals are stuck all the way around in layers until the bottom of the lantern. There one to three layers of green petals are stuck, sometimes with the petals pointing downwards. Next the lantern is placed upside down to dry. When the time comes to use the lantern, a candle is placed inside and lit – this is the magic. If you happen to visit a temple on or around Buddha's Birthday, you will be surprised to see the lanterns hanging with pieces of paper with writing on them dangling from the bottom. These pieces of paper have the names of people on them. Anyone who wants to can "buy" a lantern and write anything he or she likes on it. A donation is given to the temple. Buddhists believe that the more we give, the more generous we are, the happier we are. The money given helps the temple for its expenses as well as helping for any of the numerous welfare projects that most temples have.

Buddhists believe that the more we give, the more generous we are, the happier we are.

There are also ceremonies for marriages, births and special birthdays. Childless couples may have a ceremony in the hope of bearing a child; nervous students may chant for good exam results.

Lay Life

If anyone wishes to become a Buddhist, he often decides his own course of spiritual training, taking advice from the monk or nun he chooses as his teacher. Usually he receives the five training precepts: not to kill, not to steal, not to indulge in sexual misconduct, not to lie, and not to take intoxicants. These are not vows, but conscious decisions to train in certain areas. Failure is met with sorrow and a greater determination to try harder. Then, in order to confirm his desire to help living beings, he may later take the 48 Bodhisattva precepts. The gist of these rules is repeated at the end of every ceremony:

> "May all beings be saved.
> May all sufferings be ended.
> May we learn all Dharma teachings.
> And may we attain enlightenment.
> I vow to save all beings.
> I vow to end all sufferings.
> I vow to learn all Dharma teachings.
> I vow to attain enlightenment."

These are not vows, but conscious decisions to train in certain areas. Failure is met with sorrow and a greater determination to try harder.

Each temple has its own program. Lay people choose any temple they like and go there as often as they like. Usually they choose a temple for its beautiful position, or because some member of the family used to go there or

because they like the monks. Then they chose the program they wish to follow. There are chanting classes, text study classes, lectures, ceremonies and religious practice, bowing and reciting. There are youth groups, older people's groups, chorale groups, study groups, social work groups and groups that go on temple tours. In addition, there are possibilities for individuals to stay in a temple and do a retreat or special religious practice. The variety of activities is infinite and can be adjusted according to the wishes of the individual involved!

Chapter IV

VISITING
TEMPLES

VISITING TEMPLES

Introduction

The layout of a temple(Songgwang-sa Temple)

veryone is welcome to freely visit a Korean Buddhist temple at almost any time. In order to make a more pleasant visit, we have put together this information for you. When you tour a temple, please enjoy the beauty of these treasuries of culture, the homes of people seeking spiritual

understanding, and places where Buddhism is taught and practiced. As temples vary enormously we decided to put the information about temples into sections rather than to write a guided tour. Thus it can also be used as reference material for reading the other sectionsof the book.

We have used a variety of sources and tried our best to make the data accurate. Sources include the information boards in front of temples, Korean Buddhism, a compendium printed for the 1988 Olympics, and an article by Greta Diemente Sibley, Who's Who in Korean Iconography. We hope that you find it all useful.

There is a way to make your visit more enjoyable. Although Buddhists suffer from the normal human failings, they do try to live up to the ideals of the Buddha who taught a way of life, philosophy or religion - depending on the way you look at it - based on taking total responsibility for oneself and behaving with total tolerance towards others. Thus the monks and nuns who live in the temples try to be tolerant and open-minded, living to the best of their ability. In order for harmony to prevail, there are a few restrictions...

> Everyone is welcome to freely visit a Korean Buddhist temple at almost any time. In order to make a more pleasant visit, we have put together this information for you.

Making a Pleasant Visit

Firstly, when you come to any shrine, please either take a quick look in from the doorway and move on or take your shoes off and go into the shrine. Don't linger in the doorway as it is considered rude. If you enter, sit down for a few moments and feel the atmosphere. If there are people inside, they will be chanting, or reciting a special word or phrase with a long string of beads, or meditating. They are there because this is their main practice place and they can come at any time they wish.

Secondly, although the temple is magnificent, it is the home of the monks or nuns who live there. Although there are no restrictions to taking pictures of the exteriors of buildings, pagodas, stone lanterns etc., sometimes there are objections to taking photos inside. Ask someone with a gesture and respect their reply. Consider how you would feel being photographed in similar circumstances... Put yourself in their shoes: would you like to be photographed at breakfast (even if you eat it in such a novel way)? So, if someone makes a gesture of "NO" (don't take that picture/go in that area), please respect it.

Thirdly, if a monk, nun or layperson should stop and put his/her hands together and bow, they are greeting you. Please return the greeting by stopping and bowing, or by making the same gesture.

For Further Information

There is very little written on Korean Buddhism in general and temples in particular. However, opposite Kyongbuk Palace, behind the National Museum, there is a book shop, Pul-il, where you can buy the way of Korean Zen by one of the greatest teachers of this century, Ven. Kusan. It contains an excellent history of Korean Buddhism. Then there is Echoes

There is very little written on Korean Buddhism in general and temples in particular.

from Mt. Kaya, a straight translation of the philosophy of Ven. Songch'ol the spiritual head of the Korean Chogye Order until his death in 1993 available at Lotus Lantern. Also you can ring Sue Bae at the RAS tel. no. 763-9483 for information and especially if you want to go on one of their excellent tours.

Don' t Forget:

– to wear loose, sensible clothes so that you can sit on the floor (avoid shorts);

– to wear shoes that slip on and off easily;

– to take time to tune in to the atmosphere of the particular temple that you are visiting.

Thank you for respecting our Buddhist temples.

The Temple Compound

A Buddhist temple compound is far more than just a collection of buildings—it is a microcosm: a home to the ordained members of the Buddhist community, a shelter for people in trouble, a place for orphans and the old, as well as somewhere for students who want to do intensive studies. Built at different times under different circumstances, temples vary enormously, each one having its own special features. They do, however, follow a basic pattern.

First of all, the land is chosen according to the ancient science of geomancy which considers the shape of the mountains, position of water and the cardinal directions. Next the Main Hall is built, accompanied by special ceremonies. The other religious buildings (like shrines) follow, set out so that the visitor is carried from the mundane world of human beings, through three progressive gates, to the spiritual world of the Buddhas and Bodhisattvas. The whole arrangement, if seen from the air, forms a mandala, a cosmic pattern. Last of all the buildings necessary for the ordained members who live there are built. These include kitchens, eating areas, living places, bathing facilities and so on.

Outside the Compound

At the entrance to most temples, there is an information board which is in English at all the larger temples. It recounts the history of the temple and also alerts the visitor to associated hermitages that are beyond the main temple and, sometimes, hiking trails around that particular mountain area. It also points out special temple treasures: statues, monuments, halls. Apart from the information board, usually there are a number of free-standing, stone objects on the way to the first gate. These are monuments, including stele, pudo and pagodas.

Monuments

Monuments of various kinds are plentiful and their meaning can be guessed by their location and amount of inscription. Many lines of three Chinese characters is a listing of names of people who donated funds for building or restoration. Many characters on a stele with a turtle base will recount the history of the temple. If it is done by a famous person, there may be a separate information sign nearby, such as the one at Chikji-sa near Kimch'on by the famous philosopher-statesman, Yi Yulgok. If a stele and turtle base is near a pudo, it is a dedication to the monk whose ashes are enshrined in the pudo.

Pudo

Pudo, stone monuments to famous monks, sometimes have the sari ("jewels" or small stone-like calcified relics left after cremation — much venerated and respected by Buddhists everywhere) of the monk buried beneath them. Bulbous in shape, older or simpler ones often have small or large caps on top of them.

Pudo can be found in front, behind, or to the side of a temple complex. In Pomo-sa, in Pusan, they can easily be missed because

Pudo

You walk along a gently winding path which leads up to the first gate which is called "One Pillar" Gate.

they are so far to the side of the temple compound. In Kumsan-sa, near Kimje, they are several hundred meters beyond the compound walls. Sometimes, they are found standing alone and, it seems, forgotten in a remote area where other traces of the temple have disappeared.

The Three Gates

After passing the above mentioned objects the real tour begins. You walk along a gently winding path which leads up to the first gate which is called "One Pillar" Gate. Then you pass through the second, "Four Guardians" Gate–a two-door building. Here the four awesome protectors of the temple greet you.

Nearby is the third gate called, the "Gate of Non-duality." This gate represents the fact that, though the visitor is passing from the secular world into the spiritual world of the temple, these two worlds are not

different from one another, they are not-two, non-dual.

Somewhere before reaching the main entrance to the temple, the path crosses a bridge over a stream. This crossing is a symbolic purification.

Inside the Compound

Within the confines of the temple compound there are many different places to see. The buildings are varied and, like the kitchens, rather evident. However there are various other objects which will be totally new to the unaccustomed visitor. These include pagodas, stone lanterns, and often objects special to that temple.

Pagodas

These are usually monuments to great personalities and enshrine their ashes or calcified remains. Pagodas are said to have evolved from the dome-shaped stupas of India and now resemble multi-storied buildings with "roofs" on each level and often pilasters on the corners and sides.

The First Gate : "One Pilla"Gate
The Second Gate : "The Four Guardians Gate"
The Third Gate : "Not Two"Gate

They always have an uneven number of storeys and also once had an ornate metal finial, a decoration on the top. Sadly, the iron bars on which they were secured have deteriorated and most of the pieces have been lost. (These days, there is a fashion to replace the finial with a modern replica.).

Originally pagodas were built of wood. This can easily be seen in the older ones because the brick and later the stone subsequently used was fashioned in the same manner — as if it was wood. As time went by, brick-like stone became the common building material. A fine example of this is the pagoda at the site of Punhwang-sa, in Kyongju. The oldest and largest is the partially destroyed pagoda at the Miruk-sa site on Iksan which was built in seventh century Paekje. Although most of the extant pagodas are from the Koryo Period (916-1392), there are still many dating from the Shilla period. These pagodas stand out because of the loveliness of their proportions and the lightness, almost elegance of the design.

These lanterns are often lit so that the monks and nuns can see their way to the Main Hall for the 3 a.m. chanting ceremony.

At Sonam-sa in Songju, standing by the path to the temple together with other pudo and monuments, is a most unusual sari container. On the base sit four animals holding up a little three-storey pagoda.

Stone Lanterns

These are usually found in the main courtyard (and at royal tombs). Usually stone lanterns are made of granite, beautifully decorated with different motifs. Near the top there is a square or octagonal shaped section where the oil lamp or candle was burned; the light is diffused through four openings, one in each direction. These lanterns are often lit so that the monks and nuns can see their way to the Main Hall for the 3 a.m. chanting ceremony.

Buildings

Buildings include the Bell Pavilion; the Main Hall; one building for the Disciples; one building for the Judges; a museum; a building for the portraits of great monks; and a building for the pictures of the Buddha's life. Often there are many smaller buildings which include shrines to different Buddhas and Bodhisattvas as well as local folk gods. Then there are the monks' buildings which vary in number and size depending on the number of inhabitants and needs of the temple; occasionally there is one building unique to that temple.

Just before entering the main compound, sometimes just over the main entrance, there is a pavilion-gate. The pavilion portion above may be open or may have walls, it may be neglected or used for meetings and study or as a Bell Pavilion. The lower section is open and makes a thorough-fare to the courtyard.

The Bell Pavilion

On the way to the Main Hall, you may pass an open, two-storey structure, within which were the four instruments that call all living things to hear the words of the Buddha and which regulate the timetable of temple life.

Pagoda(Punwhang-sa, Nat'l Treasure No. 30)

Often there are many smaller buildings which include shrines to different Buddhas and Bodhisattvas as well as local folk gods.

Stone Lantern

The Main Hall

There is usually little doubt about which building is the Main Hall. Location, contents and the attention it receives separate it from the other buildings. The number of statues therein depends on the wishes and wealth of the temple, so they can range from one to at least eleven as in the Taejok-kwang-jon at Kumsan-sa in Kimje. There is generally a certain system followed in the number, disposition and personalities chosen.

The Main Hall(Taeung-jon)

The Main Hall is usually called Teung-jon or Taeungbo-jon (Great Hero Hall) and so the central figure is usually Sakyamuni, the Historical Buddha (Sokamoni-bul in Korean). However, if the Main Hall carries the name of Kuknak-jon, then the image within is always Amitabha, Buddha of the Western Paradise, (Amit'a-bul in Korean). These two Buddhas are the most popular.

However, as in Haein-sa, near Taegu, the main statue is Vairocana (Pirojana-bul in Korean), the Cosmic Buddha.

The Disciples' Hall

The Disciples' Hall is called the Nahan-jon. There statues representing specific enlightened disciples of the Buddha are to be found. The statues are usually made of wood and number between sixteen and 500 serious-looking men, often brightly dressed, seated cross-legged or on stools with hands

Another building often seen is the Yongsan-jon, named for a sacred mountain in India where the Buddha delivered the Lotus Sutra.

on legs, or holding books, or gesturing, and one is always holding a resigned tiger by the hind legs with his head and fore paws dangling. Each statue represents a disciple of the Buddha who attained enlightenment and each one has an individual story. If you look carefully, you can enjoy the humor inherent in temple life!

The Judgment Hall

At the larger temples without exception you will always find the Myongbu-jon (Judgment Hall) which contains Ksitigarbha, the Bodhisattva of the Suffering (Chijang Posal in Korean) his two attendants, Modukkuiwang, a wise man and cousin of the Buddha, and Tomyong-jonja, a disciple, as well as the Ten Judges who determine one's fate after death according to the deeds performed during life. The Ten Judges may be statues, rarely

portraits only, but often there is a combination with pictures depicting the punishments of wrongdoers. Around the judges are errand boys to carry writing brushes and paper; near the door are messengers; and just inside the doorway, two ferocious, ready-to-strike guards. One attendant holds a box which contains the keys to paradise. Usually, too, there will be a mirror somewhere. This is actually the instrument of Yama, the God of Death who shows us a reflection of ourselves so that we may judge ourselves, for we know what we have done.

The Museum

Most of the large temples have a museum. There, ancient and valuable objects are stored and made available to visitors at special times.

Smaller Buildings

Another building often seen is the Yongsan-jon, named for a sacred mountain in India where the Buddha delivered the Lotus Sutra. Within is found Sakyamuni

The inside of the Judgment Hall

Buddha with numerous nahan (Arahants: enlightened disciples of the Buddha). The total number ranges from sixteen to 500.

Portraits of special monks are in the Pyochung-won in larger temples and in the Main Hall in smaller temples.

Halls for the secondary Buddhas and Bodhisattvas are often named according to the statue that they house. Piro-jon is the small shrine housing the Vairocana Buddha, the Cosmic Buddha. The Yaksa-jon is for the Universal Healer, Yaksayorae. Miruk-jon is for the Future Buddha, Maitreya (Miruk-bul in Korean). The Kwannum-jon is important as it houses Avalokitesvara, the Bodhisattva of Compassion (Kwan-seum Posal in Korean) a source of succor for all who suffer.

The Palang-jon, another building at larger temples, honors the eight important events in the life of the Buddha with large murals. These are often very magnificent and sometimes old and celebrated, as in Haein-sa.

The Monks' Buildings

The living quarters, guest rooms, kitchens and eating hall are usually a little off to one side of the compound. In larger temples, there is also a study hall where monks live while learning the basic texts and chants. And there is almost always a meditation hall, at least in larger temples, carefully built in the quietest corner of the temple compound. These days, because there are so many visitors, there may a cafeteria-type eating place where anyone is welcome to come and eat at the meal times.

Iconography

Here are some basic indications of the different characters figuring in Korean Buddhist Iconography.

Statues

The table on the following page gives the names of the principle statues in Sanskrit, Korean and English. In the text, we have stuck to Sanskrit names because more people are familiar with them and they are less confusing.

Guardians

Whether they be mighty wooden statues or paintings housed in gates, or simply two figures painted on doors, the first personalities to be encountered at a Korean temple are generally the Four Guardians.

If the temple one is visiting is not particularly grandiose, it is usually the two gate gods one must pass in order to enter the temple grounds. These deities prevent evil spirits from entering the temple precincts. In China they are called Heng and Ha. They boast the power to send forth deadly rays of light, one from his nostrils giving forth the sound "heng," the other from his mouth with the sound "ha." The mouth is the door of the face, and, symbolically, Ha's open mouth indicates that the temple is protected whether the doors are opened or closed. The two gods protect on another level as well, that of

Sakyamuni Buddha(Woljong-sa Temple)

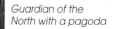

*Guardian of the
North with a pagoda*

*Samantabhadra Bodhisattva
on an elephant*

wisdom over ignorance.

In the larger Korean temples, one is likely to find, in addition to the two gate gods painted on the doors, the Four Guardians housed in their own gate structure. In statue or painted form, these figures are imposing, often as much as five meters tall.

These protectors are of Hindu origin, and are said to have helped Siddhartha Gautama, the Indian prince who became the Buddha, to leave his father's house on the night of his renunciation by each taking hold of one hoof of Siddhartha's horse and

*Guardian of the
West with a sword*

lifting him over the palace walls. In another legend, Siddhartha (now the Buddha Sakyamuni, the Silent One of the Sakya Clan) was setting out on his alms round. The guardians all rushed to present him with bowls made of precious stones. The Buddha refused them. The guardians then offered him bowls of ordinary stone. Accepting them as more suitable to his position, Sakyamuni piled the four one atop another, and miraculously, they became one vessel. The guardians served Siddhartha throughout his earthly life.

Guardian of the South carrying a lute

Manjusri Bodhisattva on a lion

Guardian of the East with a dragon

The Four Guardians all bear a fierce countenance and trample the opponents of Buddhism under their feet. Each of them represents one of the cardinal directions.

The guardian of the North, Tamun Chonwang, holds a pagoda, or tower. The tower represents a reliquary stupa, symbolizing death. The stupa consists of three basic parts: the base, which represents the earth, the dome, which represents heaven, and a connecting piece, or cosmic axis.

Chonjang Chonwang is the guardian of the southern quarter. One may identify him by the sword he bears, usually poised for action. He is reputed to have the power to multiply his sword so that he can always outnumber his opponents.

Chigook Chonwang guards the East. He is easily spotted by the lute he holds, the strings of which control wind, thunder, hail and other weather phenomena.

The guardian of the West, Kwangmok Chonwang, holds a dragon in one hand and a jewel in the other. The original meaning of these symbols seems to be lost in time.

The Four Guardians should be looked for in the corners of temple murals where variations may be observed between Koryo and Choson style painting, for even within the history of Korean Buddhism the objects which the guardians hold have changed. (Which guardian governs which quarter of the world is often disputed.)

Regardless of iconographic variations, one may identify the guardians by their ever-present battle dress and imposing facial expres-sions. Their variety in appearance only serves to provoke thought and make us more aware of their function. They forever remain routers of evil demons and protectors of Buddhism and the Buddha's teachings.

Buddhas & Bodhisattvas

Most of the other statues which one sees in the temples are either Buddhas, enlightened beings, or Bodhisattvas who are beings who have given themselves to helping others. Most of the Bodhisattvas represent one particular aspect of either wisdom or compassion while the Buddhas are the embodiment of perfect wisdom and perfect compassion.

Buddha Sakyamuni
(Sokamoni-bul, in Korean)

The Buddha Sakyamuni is the main statue in most temples. He is the historical Buddha, the Sambhogakaya. He was born as a prince called Siddhartha Gautama in northeastern India in the fifth century BCE. Frequently, pictures of various episodes from his life will be found on the exterior of the Main Hall. Sometimes these pictures are housed sepa-rately, sometimes they are found in the back of the Main Hall (Haein-sa). One may follow Siddhartha through the process which brought him to enlightenment. Often pictured are: his mother, Queen Maya, having the auspicious dream of a white elephant; his birth in the Lumbini Garden; his childhood bath in the fire of nine dragons; his meditation in the Himalayas; his struggle with desires; his enlightenment under the Bodhi Tree; scenes of him teaching, and his death.

The mudra, hand position, of "calling the earth to witness" which is most often associated with the Buddha Sakyamuni,

The Buddha Sakyamuni is the main statue in most temples. He is the historical Buddha, the Sambhogakaya.

recalls a story about the Buddha (it is found in the Sokkur-am statue in Kyongju). Just after his enlightenment, he was challenged as to his right to sit on the small piece of ground that he was occupying. He called the earth to witness his many good deeds of past lives and so justified his seat in that place. The figure is of a seated Buddha, the right hand hanging over the knee, palm inward, sometimes pointing with one finger, usually with the whole hand, towards the earth.

> He called the earth to witness his many good deeds of past lives and so justified his seat in that place.

Vairocana Buddha (Pirojana-bul, in Korean)

Vairocana is the Cosmic Buddha who spreads the light of Buddhist Truth in every direction, the Buddha who embodies the Wisdom of Universal Law. He is the center, Buddha Incarnate, the Original Teacher, the Dharmakaya. Vairocana is the embodiment of Truth and Knowledge. As is the case with all Buddhas and Bodhisattvas, Vairocana is not exclusive of other Buddhas but represents a particular aspect of Buddhahood: in this case, the aspect of Cosmic Energy.

Buddhas & Bodhisattvas

Sanskrit	Korean	English
Sakyamuni	Sokamoni-bul	Historical Buddha
Amitabha	Amita-bul	Buddha of Infinite Light
Vairocana	Pirojana-bul	Buddha of Cosmic Energy
Bhaisagya	Yaksayorae-bul	Buddha of Healing Medicine Buddha
Avalokitesvara	Kwanseum Posal	Compassion Bodhisattva
Ksitigarbha	Chijang Posal	Bodhisattva of Suffering
Mahastamprapta	Taesaeji Posal	Bodhisattva of Power
Manjusri	Moonsoo Posal	Bodhisattva of Wisdom
Samanatabhadra	Pohyun Posal	Bodhisattva of Action
	Tongjin Posal (with wings on hat)	Bodhisattva of Protectin the Dharma

Vairocana Buddha

Vairocana is the Cosmic Buddha who spreads the light of Buddhist Truth in every direction, the Buddha who embodies the Wisdom of Universal Law.

Vairocana is usually depicted with his hands in one of several positions. A common example is the mudra of the "knowledge fist." This mudra is made up of the right-hand "diamond fist" and the left-hand "diamond finger." The "diamond fist" is formed by making a tight fist with the thumb at the center. The "diamond finger" is the left index which is inserted into the right fist. The mudra of the "knowledge fist" dispels darkness. One of Vairocana's names is Diamond Buddha. The diamond represents the supreme strength and durability of Buddhist knowledge. The left index finger represents the world of sentient beings, the surrounding right hand, the protection of the world of Buddhas. Generally the left hand refers to the passive pole and the right hand to the active pole. The left represents the physical plane and the right the metaphysical. This mudra is a divine representation of the passions, and a comment on the intensity with which one aspiring to wisdom pursues the goal. The mudra represents the union of the sexes with Vairocana as the procreator. Other mudras of Vairocana are variations on the joining of the hands, palm to palm, fingers crossed over one another and thumbs erect, or the right hand encompassing the left hand which has been closed in on itself. These mudra also represent the universal knowledge of the Buddha.

Vairocana is sometimes enshrined in his own building called the Great Light Hall. He is usually unattended when in his own shrine. In other halls, he is the central figure of a trinity. He is often attended by Manjusri and Samantabhadra.

Amitabha Buddha
(Amit' a-bul in Korean)

Amitabha Buddha emanates from the meditation of the primordial Buddha; he is the Nirmanakaya. He is the Buddha of Infinite Light and governs the Pure land, the Western Paradise. In India, where Buddhism began, people felt relief from the extreme heat of the day when the sun reached the western sky. Thus, Amitabha's paradise came to be associated with the west. Appropriately, he sometimes wears the color red.

Amitabha has vowed to save all beings who call on him. He assists them by admitting them to his Pure Land where they will know no hindrances to achieving enlightenment. The Pure Land is no different from the Pure Mind, the state in which one is free from illusion.

Sometimes it is almost impossible to know if one is looking at a figure of Amitabha or Sakyamuni because their faces are so similar and their symbolic hand gestures are often the same. Each is generally depicted as the central figure of a triad. When trying to discriminate between the two, it is helpful to identify the images which flank the central figure. For example, if the side figures are Avalokitesvara and Mahastamprapta (Taesaeji Posal, in Korean) the Bodhisattva of Power, the central Buddha is Amitabha. If there is a separate building for this triad, then it is called the Temple of Supreme Bliss. Amitabha often holds his left hand in the "fulfilling the vow" pose, the palm turned outward in a gesture of offering. This pose is found most commonly in standing figures. When he is seated, the left palm is often simply held face upward in the lap. The right hand is raised, a gesture of fearlessness. Three forms of this right hand gesture are: the thumb touching the index, middle, or ring finger. The thumb and index finger form a circle which represents the perfection of wisdom.

> Bhaisagya Buddha is the Universal Healer or Medicine Buddha. He provides relief not only from disease and misfortune, but also from ignorance, which is the greatest ill to Buddhists.

Bhaisagya Buddha
(Yaksayorae-bul, in Korean)

Bhaisagya Buddha is the Universal Healer or Medicine Buddha. He provides relief not only from disease and misfortune, but also from ignorance, which is the greatest ill to Buddhists.

Usually Bodhisattvas, not Buddhas, hold attribute objects. The alms bowl and the medicine bowl (which evolved as a symbol from the alms bowl) are the only exceptions. Sakyamuni and Amitabha hold the alms bowl, or sometimes hold their hands in a mudra suggestive of holding the vessel, and Bhaisagya Buddha holds the medicine bowl.

The alms bowl is one of the very few personal possessions of Buddhist monks. It represents the sincere offerings of believers and the humility of monks.

Images of Bhaisagya Buddha closely resemble those of Amitabha except that the latter is usually golden, while the former is almost always white. Though Bhaisagya Buddha usually holds the medicine bowl in both hands, he sometimes holds it in only one hand, the left. In this case, the right hand assumes the pose of the "absence of fear" which, although certainly appropriate to his role as a healer, is usually associated with Amitabha.

Maitreya Buddha
(Miruk-bul, in Korean)

Maitreya Buddha is the Future Buddha. He lives in the Tusita Heaven where he waits until his time to be born on this earth arrives. He is the embodiment of love and

compassion.

Paintings of Maitreya are virtually nonexistent, but statues of him are still extant. They were particularly popular during the days of the Three Kingdoms (before 668 CE) and devotees carried miniatures of this Buddha in their pockets.

The Korean form of Maitreya is very special and unusual. Most people know the jolly, fat, laughing Buddha of Chinese iconography. He is the Chinese Maitreya, promising plenty in the future. The Korean counterpart is thin and easily identified when in the "posture of reflection." He sits with his right elbow resting on his right knee. His right foot or ankle is on his left knee. The left hand rests on the right ankle or foot. His head is slightly inclined, suggesting contemplation. The index and middle fingers of his right hand are slightly inflected and just touch the face. (The statue in the National Museum is hauntingly beautiful and well worth a visit.)

Many large statues in Korea are called Miruk-bul, Maitreya Buddha, but there is speculation about their true identity.

Maitreya Buddha is the Future Buddha. He lives in the Tusita Heaven where he waits until his time to be born on this earth arrives. He is the embodiment of love and compassion.

Bodhisattvas Avalokitesvara (Kwanseum Posal, in Korean)

Avalokitesvara is the Bodhisattva of Compassion. Although in India, Avalokitesvara is clearly male, she is most often depicted as neither male nor female or female by today's artists. A bit of mustache is visible in some contemporary paintings, but these works are generally of an old style. In her Buddhist context, Avalokitesvara's sex is irrelevant, the idea is an artistic impression of the idea of perfect compassion.

Born from a ray of light emanating from Amitabha's right eye, Avalokitesvara is thus closely related to Amitabha and so assists those who request access to the Pure Land. The name means "Hearer of Cries," and she is often pictured with her head slightly inclined as if listening to the pleas of the suffering. She is frequently pictured

Avalokitesvara

Tongjin. the protecter of the Dharma

Sakyamuni and Bhaisagya Buddha, composing the Trinity of the Preciousness of the Teachings.

Paintings

Guardian Painting
(Shinjung Taengwha, in Korean)

The Shinjung Taengwha, a painting featuring Tongjin Posal, is commonly found in Korean temples. Its frequent presence, however, in no way seems to make its meaning well-known. The only point on which most people agree, Buddhists included, is that they don't know much about the Shinjung Taengwha.

There are twelve to twenty figures depicted in the Shinjung Taengwha. The central image is of Tongjin Posal, who is easily identi-fied by his elaborate headdress which resembles a fan of feathers. One of a number of beings who guard the doctrine, Tongjin Posal is the Bodhisattva who protects the Saddharma-pundarika, the Lotus Sutra of the True Law, one of the most revered Mahayana texts which explains that the truth is conveyed by silence and gestures as well as words.

There are different interpretations of the Shinjung Taengwha. One is that the figures surrounding Tongjin represent beings who are well-acquainted with the Three Refuges: the Buddha, his teaching (Dharma), and the Buddhist community (Sangha). Another is that the figures are historical personages such as Confucius, or lesser deities like the Kitchen God. The four, or

The central image is of Tongjin Posal, who is easily identi-fied by his elaborate headdress which resembles a fan of feathers.

The Dragon King

Shinjung Taengwha

As belief in mountain spirits preceded Buddhism's entry into Korea, Sanshin is not of Buddhist origin but was absorbed into Buddhism.

sometimes five, figures at the base of the painting or to the sides of Tongjin Posal, are clearly guardians. One guardian often carries a rolled-up scroll, representing the doctrine which he protects.

Depending on the size of the temple, and consequently on the number of halls or shrines therein, the Shinjung Taengwha is found in any one of many buildings, but most often on the right wall of the Main Hall.

It is interesting to note that, as the gods are beings in the realm of pleasure, they cannot attain enlightenment. Therefore the monks and nuns turn to the Taenghwa when they chant the Heart Sutra in order to help the gods attain a human birth in their next life and so reach enlightenment. In addition, as humans need help from the gods, often people will bow towards the Taenghwa as a gesture of respect and humility in the understanding of the fact that it is difficult to reach attainment alone.

The Mountain God (Sanshin, in Korean)

Every Korean temple has a place for Sanshin, the Mountain God, whether it be a painting and small altar set up in one of the larger halls, or, as is most often the case, a small separate building off in one corner of the compound. Sanshin is not depicted in statue form, but instead is always painted.

As belief in mountain spirits preceded Buddhism's entry into Korea, Sanshin is not of Buddhist origin but was absorbed into Buddhism. Little by little it came to be suggested that Sanshin had been a Bodhisattva all along.

Sanshin is particularly popular among women hoping for sons. However, visitors to most temples pay their respects to Sanshin.

The paintings of the Mountain God all follow the same basic pattern. Pictured is an old man seated with, or sometimes on, a tiger. Because tigers were a constant threat in mountainous areas, their ferocity came to be associated with powerful spirits. The Mountain God is not exclu-sively the old man or the tiger, rather he is both. Perhaps the tiger's presence also suggests the close relationship in geomancy between mountains and tigers.

Commonly the old man and tiger are pictured in a deep valley with a stone cliff on the right.

The Recluse (Toksong-in, in Korean)

Toksong-in is commonly known as the Recluse. Toksong-in is not an historicalpersonage or a paradigm of isolation. He represents in the Mahayana tradition of Buddhism what the arhant represents in the Theravada. The arhant is a holy person, perfect being, a disciple of the Buddha Sakyamuni. Toksong-in is a

Chilsong, the Big Dipper, has roots in Taoism and Shamanism.

timeless being, a reminder that one should not seek enlightenment outside of oneself, for, "alone and holy," he is enlightened within.

Mahayanists are wary of the illusion of the ego appropriating external self-definitions. Toksong-in urges us to seek the Buddha within, to realize that everything is inside of us and not external to us. Demonstrating Chinese iconographic and cultural influence, a young manservant is sometimes present holding tea, a platter of fruit, or a fan.

Chisong-gak

The Big Dipper (Chilsong, in Korean)

Chilsong, the Big Dipper, has roots in Taoism and Shamanism. The Great Bear Constellation, which is Chilsong, is visible year round, partly accounting for the great reverence with which he is regarded. Chilsong is thought to control both good and bad fortune. He is particu-larly popular among women hoping for children.

On the left hand side of the Main Hall or the Judgement Hall, a large painting of Chilsong is sometimes hung. The painting is colorful and impressive. It contains many figures and festive scenes. Presumably, when Buddhism came to Korea, people assumed that they were a manifestation of the compassionate Buddha. Seven Buddhas,

one for each star, run in a row along the top of the painting. The seven stars pictured as Buddhas demonstrate the incorporation of originally Shaman concepts into Korean Buddhism.

Some large Korean temples have an entire shrine dedicated to Chilsong. In this case Chilsong is depicted economically in one statue. Like Bhaisagya Buddha, he holds a medicine cup in his left palm which rests on his left knee. In his other hand he sometimes holds a lotus flower. In addition to the statue, he is further depicted in seven paintings, one of each star deity, which are found on the walls of the shrine. In keeping with Chilsong's celestial nature, to the left and right, respectively, of the central Chilsong, are figures of Ilgwang and Wolgwang. Ilgwang's crown has at its center a red sun, Wolgwang's, a white moon. Both hold lotuses.

The Oxherding Pictures

On the outer walls of the Main Hall, along with the paintings depicting the life of the Buddha Sakyamuni and other pictures, there are often the ten Oxherding Pictures (called Shim-oo-do in Korean). Coming from the Sung Dynasty (1126-1279) in China, they were con-ceived by Buddhist masters as a teaching device. The pictures represent the training of the mind by the metaphor of tethering an ox; the herder is you, the ox is your mind.

The progressive whitening of the ox indicates the gradual awakening of the oxherd to his true nature; it is a process of purification. The original series ended with an empty circle, for it was inherently understood that the ox herder carried on with life as usual, now an enlightened life. In an effort to dispel the frequent misunderstanding of Buddhism's "enlightenment" as mere emptiness, the series was expanded to include the oxherd's return to the world.

Searching for the Ox illustrates the separation of the herder and the ox, and the former's seeming violation of his true nature. The oxherd is dissatisfied with his environment, he is subject to passions, and

desire for possessing a satisfactory self-definition and fear of losing that identity have him in a vulnerable position and a painful predicament.

Seeing the Footprints illustrates the awareness gained by the oxherd that there is the possibility of transcending his pain. He has a preliminary understanding of the origin of his pain. Though he is unable to see the ox, the ox's presence is known.

Perceiving the Ox illustrates the oxherd's realization that nothing exists outside of himself, and, therefore, that "himself" as an individual entity is non-existent. He is comforted by the loss of objective perception. The herder is free from the need to defend his objective self-definition.

Catching the Ox illustrates the struggle which is the result of incompletely transcending aggression. The oxherd has laid hands on the ox, but has not developed the energy to keep it under his control. He knows his ego to be untrue, but the ego (attempting objectification of the self) struggles to control the herder.

Taming the Ox illustrates the oxherd's determined and concentrated efforts to attain wisdom despite his still prevalent vulnerability to confusion, for the ox and herder are not yet one. The herder must keep his whip ready to prevent the ox from wandering, just as the student of Zen must discipline himself to prevent his mind from wandering.

The properly tended ox is pacified. When the fuel of the passions is burned up, the fire is forgotten. The oxherd is pictured Riding the Ox Home. The oxherd's concentration is not subject to the calls of the world. His mind may no longer be deceived, but instead has begun to engage in truly creative activity. He may not be led astray. With a joyful heart, he meanders home.

The Ox Transcended/The Oxherd Alone illustrates that the ox was never real. Not only has the ego no chance of gaining control, but there is no longer even a notion

of an individual mind to be deluded by the ego. The light of wisdom shines. The oxherd is no longer born, and no longer dies, the phenomena that previously caused so much pain. He is unborn.

The Ox and Herder Transcended, illustrated by the empty circle, shows only the slightest remaining distance, which is yet an infinite separation, between mind and self.

With the nonexistence of dualism, Buddhism cannot be exclusive or inclusive. At this point, it is not a path to be followed, but a truth to be lived. The oxherd no longer follows, but knows the immediacy of wisdom.

Reaching the Origin, one is not enriched by anything external. It is apparent that one was never in fact enriched, but was eternally pure and compassionate. There is only a "source" or "origin" in the sense of eternally present, inexhaustible, serenity.

In the World, the awakened, enlightened being follows no example. He is what he knows to be true and projects his Buddha-nature to those who need his care.

Eight Scenes of the Life of the Buddha

Paintings of the eight scenes of the life of Buddha can be found in the Palsong-jon, the Eight Pictures Hall, or on the outside walls of the Main Hall of Buddhist Temples. When inside, they are skillfully artistic and colorful as well as quite complex. In addition to the specific episodes, associated ones are shown and the background of the scene is elaborated. When on the outside walls, they are of simple design in a more naive style. In either case, there are eight clues by which each can be identified: (1) elephant; (2) baby; (3) sick or dead man; (4) white horse over a wall; (5) starved figure; (6) tempters; (7) halo; (8) bier.

(Elephant)—
Announcement of the imminent birth

A white elephant is a sacred, auspicious symbol in India, where the Buddha was born, and is depicted as the vehicle that brought to earth the Buddha-to-be. Between the right ribs he entered Maya's womb.In more detailed indoor paintings, the background is of the palace in which he was born with many people in the rooms and gardens. A whole host of heavenly beings surround the elephant and the Buddha-to-be in a cloud that trails to earth above Maya's head.

(Baby)—The birth

The well-developed babe emerged from the right side of a fully clothed mother and began walking immediately after birth. He was born into a royal family and bore the title of Prince. He was named Siddhartha; Gautama was his family name. Seven days after his birth his mother died. At sixteen he married and had a son. His life in the palace was one of comfort and luxury.

In compound pictures there are nine dragons washing the baby with many earthly attendants.

(Sick/dead man)—
The world outside the palace

Eventually Siddhartha began to see, outside the sanctuary of the palace, sickness, old age and death. Then he saw a recluse

The birth of the Buddha

The enlightenment of the Buddha

The first teaching

and realized that the only way to overcome sickness, old age and death was to leave home and attain enlightenment. Siddhartha decided to leave his family and home for solitude and meditation.

In the simple pictures one emaciated body tells the story. In the complex ones, life goes on as usual in the palace, but outside the walls in the lower right can be seen illness and in the lower left, death.

Enlightenment smile of his disciple

(White horse over wall)— Renunciation

His father, learning of Siddhartha's intentions to leave the palace, placed extra guards by the gates and others to watch over his son at all times. But Siddhartha, with the aid of the four guardians and other spirits, was able to escape over the wall on his favorite white horse.

A white horse taking to the air, with his master astride it and the groom hanging on to the tail, represents renunciation.

(Starved figure)—Asceticism

For six years he studied and meditated. As was the custom in those days, he punished and disciplined the body until he was nearly dead. Finally realizing that this was not the right way, he began to live moderately and to maintain a healthy body in order to practice in his quest for understanding and enlightenment.

(Tempters)—Temptations

The demon Mara sought to break the spirit of the meditating man and sent various lures away from the path Siddhartha had chosen. First he sent worldly pleasures. When these failed, he sent his army-cum-monsters but the power

Passing away(Nirvana)

of the nearly enlightened Buddha was able to stop them and turn their weapons into lotus blossoms. Evil, in the guise of Mara and his tricks, was defeated and righteousness prevailed.

The three voluptuous women trying to seduce him leave no doubt that this is the temptation scene!

(Halo)—Enlightenment

After overcoming temptation, enlightenment is complete. Siddhartha had become the historical Buddha, Sakyamuni. For forty-five years, he wandered and taught anyone who was interested in his understanding of reality.

In addition to the halo there are disciples at his feet, but in the complex pictures this scene is subordinated by a confusing array of celestial and worldly beings and structures.

(Bier)—Death

At the age of eighty the Buddha died. His disciples and many animals gathered around the bier to mourn his passing. In elaborate paintings, there is a colorful shower of relics from the burning casket. Around the body are crowds of both heavenly and earthly mourners.

Conclusion

Please don't fall into the trap of thinking that all temples are the same; they are not. Each one has distinctive characteristics and a different story. Having visited a few and worked out the basic structure, you can start to concentrate on the individuality and appreciate the finer points of each setting, each building, and each painting or statue. But don't be in a hurry, there are over 2,000 temples in Korea, not to mention innumerable hermitages!

Chapter V

THE MAIN TEMPLES OF THE KOREAN BUDDHIST CHOGYE ORDER

THE MAIN TEMPLES OF THE KOREAN BUDDHIST CHOGYE ORDER

Korea has many large temples. Here is some basic information about the main ones. First we will consider three special temples which represent the Three Jewels of Buddhism. These are: T'ongdo-sa Temple, representing the Buddha; Haein-sa Temple, representing the teaching; and Song-gwang-sa Temple representing the Buddhist community. Then we will cover other major temples of interest and finish up with a few temples in Seoul which, though often not as grand as those in the mountains are, nonetheless, well worth visiting.

The Three Jewels Temples

The Temple Without a Buddha Statue: T'ongdo-sa

One of Korea's greatest monks, Master Chajang, brought relics of the Buddha with him and these he enshrined at T'ongdo-sa Temple.

T'ongdo-sa, "Pass into Enlightenment," Temple is the first of the "Three Jewels" temples of Korea representing the Buddha. It is traditionally a Zen Temple and as far as the number of buildings is concerned, 65, it is the largest temple in Korea.

T'ongdo-sa Temple, once a center of Korean Buddhism, was built in 646, in the reign of Queen Sondok by Master Chajang on his return from China. One of Korea's greatest monks, Master Chajang, brought relics of the Buddha with him and these he enshrined at T'ongdo-sa Temple.

Offering Table and Dharma-Teaching Sit in the Main Hall looking out on the Stupa (T'ongdo-sa temple)

The Main Hall is
unique in that it has
no statue, only a
window looking out
to a stupa. The
ceiling of the hall is
especially
marvelous as it is
covered with a
beautifully executed
pattern of
chrysanthemums.

Master Chajang, coming from a royal family, could have advanced well in the court; instead he chose to be a monk. The king, appreciating his abilities, continued to request him to accept a court position which he refused. In exasperation, the king threatened the monk with the death penalty if he refused again. Master Chajang calmly replied, "I would rather die keeping the laws of the Buddha for one day than live for one hundred years breaking them." Seeing the wisdom of this reply, the king permitted Master Chajang to continue his monk's life.

Master Chajang went to China with ten other monks in 636. There he received relics of the Buddha from Manjusri Bodhisattva and then returned to Shilla with different sets of texts. He built a small hermitage on Yongjuk-san Mountain and from there oversaw the building of T'ongdo-sa.

Before entering the temple compound, the visitor has to pass over the "windless" bridge which leads into a forest of "windless" pines. Most temples have a bridge - often over a wonderful rushing torrent - before the gates to the compound. This is a symbolic purification of the individual as he or she passes from the secular world into the spiritual world.

The Main Hall at T'ongdo-sa Temple, (National Treasure No. 144), was reconstructed in 1601 in the reign of King Sonjo; the previous one had been destroyed in the Hideyoshi Invasion. It is one of the only ancient buildings (with the Great Hall of Light) in the temple compound. The Main Hall is unique in that it has no statue, only a window looking out to a stupa. The ceiling of the hall is especially marvelous as it is covered with a beautifully executed pattern of chrysanthemums.

Behind the Main Hall is the Diamond Precepts platform. On the platform is a bell-shaped stupa or pagoda, surrounded by a stone barrier. The gate to enter into this little enclosure is very finely decorated with dragons, clouds and two protector guardians which have been hewn out of the granite doors. At the four corners of the platform there are protective deities. This bell-shaped stupa is perfectly proportioned. The base and upper part are decorated with lotus patterns, lotus blossoms, lotus petals, the Four Virtues and gods; it is believed to enshrine the relics of the Buddha which Master Chajang brought from

*The Diamond Precepts Platform
(T'ongdo-sa temple, Nat'l Treasure
No. 290)*

China and is therefore the focal point of the temple. As the stupa contains relics of the Buddha, it represents the Buddha and so there is no need for a statue in the Main Hall as well.

The Diamond Precpts Platform (T'ongdo-sa temple, Nat'l Treasure No. 290)

Pagodas developed from stupas, the symbol used to represent the presence of the Buddha after his death because they enshrined his remains. After the Buddha was cremated, his remains were divided up between the eight different clans who had been his followers during his lifetime and each clan built a stupa. These cupola-shaped structures, being symbols of the Buddha, then continued to be constructed in the grounds of every new temple which came into being and their shape evolved as Buddhism was accepted in other cultures. As time went by, they were used to enshrine the remains of great monks as well. In China, the stupa evolved into a pagoda which also took on different forms. Today you can see pudo, bell-shaped pagodas, many-storied pagodas and simple, few storied pagodas all varying in shape, design and decoration depending on the period in which they were made, the amount of money offered by the donor and the skill of the craftsman.

There are many buildings at T'ongdo-sa. Of special interest are: the museum which contains many precious ancient objects; the memorial shrine to Chajang built in 1727 containing a portrait of the master; and the Great Hall of Light. This last is a hall dedicated to Vairocana Buddha and was constructed 600 years ago; it is reputed to be the oldest in Korea. The statue and decorations are magnificent.

Of note is the lovely Nine Dragons Pond. Originally it was very large and nine dragons lived in it. However, after some time it was reduced in size and now the monks who live in the temple believe there is only one dragon (referred to as a snake) which never comes out...There are many small hermitages in the valleys behind the temple.

The Temple of the Teaching: Haein-sa

Haein-sa Temple is the second of the Three Jewels Temples, representing the Teaching. "Haein" means "reflection on a smooth sea." It is the description of a state of meditation (samadhi) taken from the Avatamsaka Sutra. In this sutra, Haein Samadhi is a stage in which an enlightened person sees everything as it is: a world in which all dualities cease. Such a world has a surface like

Interior of the Biro-jon(Haein-sa temple)

that of a calm sea. This total tranquility, unperturbed by the vicissitudes of life, is the stage of the Buddhas and it is also our True Nature.

At first a hermitage, the temple was built by Master Sunung and Master Ichong on their return from studying in China in 802 under directions from a grateful king.

The queen of King Aejang (r. 800-809) became ill with a tumor. The king asked Master Sunung and Master Ichong to help her. They tied one end of a piece of string to the tumor, the other to a tree and chanted special verses. Miraculously, as the tumor withered, the tree died. Out of gratitude for the monks' services, the king built Haein-sa Temple. Later the temple was greatly enlarged.

There are many stories associated with Haein-sa. One of these stories happened during the Korean War. At that time, many guerrillas hid in Haein-sa and so the order was given for the temple to be bombed. The pilot flew over the buildings, trying to judge where best to drop his bomb. As he gazed down at the beautiful pattern created by the juxtaposition of the magnificent halls, he could not bring himself to destroy such a lovely place. He was court-marshaled and imprisoned. After the war, however, he became a national hero.

After passing through the three gates, there is a large courtyard. On the left is a new building, built for teaching

> "Haein" means "reflection on a smooth sea." It is the description of a state of meditation (samadhi) taken from the Avatamsaka Sutra. In this sutra,

Entrance to the Library(Haein-sa temple)

and sheltering some of the many people who come to ceremonies and festivals. On the right is the large Bell Pavilion. Continuing on up the next flight of stairs, you arrive in a courtyard in front of the Main Hall. The Main Hall was constructed in 1818 on the foundations of the one built by Master Sunung and Master Ichong. Inside, there are seven statues, from the left they are: 1) an iron Avalokitesvara, 2) a wooden Manjusri, 3) a wooden Vairocana which was formerly the principal statue before the present main statue was installed, 4) Vairocana, the principal statue

Some of the Wooden Blocks in the library(Haein-sa temple, UNESCO the World Heritage, Nat'l Treasure No. 32)

made in 1769, 5) a wooden Ksitigarbha, 6) a wooden Samantabhadra, and 7) an iron Popgi Bodhisattva (an unusual Bodhisattva known as "Born of Truth" in English).

The wooden Vairocana, the Manjusri and the Samantabhadra statues were all carved from a big ginkgo tree during the Koryo Dynasty. There are many paintings in the hall. Ich'adon with the white blood spurting out of his neck, Wonhyo and Uisang as well as other great masters are to be seen. The elaborate carvings are typical of the Choson Dynasty.

Another special feature is the paintings of the Buddha's life. These are found behind the main statues, to the left, and are highly detailed and rather unusual.

Behind the main shrine, up a steep flight of granite stairs, are two long buildings, National Treasure No. 52, which house the wood-blocks of the Tripitaka Koreana, the Buddhist texts. Constructed in 1488, the buildings escaped the fires which burnt down the rest of the temple in 1817.

The Tripitaka Koreana, National Treasure No. 32, was originally carved in the 11th century in a temple on Kanghwa Island. It was believed that the possession of these wood-blocks would protect the country against invasion — ironically, the blocks themselves were later burnt by invaders, the Mongols! In the 13th century a new set was undertaken at the orders of King Kojong (r. 1213-1259) and these were transported from Kanghwa Island on the heads of nuns to Haein-sa for safe-keeping.

The manufacturing process usually accepted is:
* the wood used is white birch;
* for three years it is submerged in sea-water;
* for three years it is boiled in sea-water;
* for three years it is dried in the shade.

It took about 16 years to carve the 52,330,152 characters on the 81,258 blocks and, because of the uniformity of the carving, it is believed that the work was done by one man. When printed, there are about 6,791 large, Chinese-style volumes.

At present an average 220 monks and novices live within the temple compound. During the meditation seasons, three months in winter and three months in summer, the number increases. Around Haein-sa there are 15 hermitages where about 200 women live. There are also a few men's hermitages. In all, as the monk who gave the

> It took about 16 years to carve the 52,330,152 characters on the 81,258 blocks and, because of the uniformity of the carving, it is believed that the work was done by one man. When printed, there are about 6,791 large, Chinese-style volumes.

The Main Hall
(Songgwang-sa temple)

information put it, there are about 500 "mountain men" living in and around Haein-sa. The temple is the largest in Korea in terms of residents and it has the largest monks' university.

Surrounded by magnificent mountains, Haein-sa Temple draws thousands of visitors from all over the world every year.

The Temple of the (Sangha) Followers: Songgwang-sa

Songgwang-sa, "Spreading Pine Temple," on Mount Chogye-san, is the third of the Three Jewels Temples, representing the Buddha's followers: monks and laity.

Songgwang-sa, "Spreading Pine Temple," on Mount Chogye-san, is the third of the Three Jewels Temples, representing the Buddha's followers: monks and laity. Many famous monks have lived here. Therefore there is a formidable collection of stele and pagodas containing the ashes of some of these masters. The most famous resident monk was Master Chinul (1158-1210). He was responsible for building up the temple.

In 1190, Master Chinul realized his life-long wish to create a situation in which like-minded people could live and practice Buddhism together. His group was called the "Concentration and Wisdom Community." For seven years they lived in a small temple but, as the community

There he built a small hermitage on Mount Chogye-san which he expanded to accommodate his growing community and it became known as Kilsang-sa and eventually Songgwang-sa.

grew, Master Chinul looked for the ideal place to move to. In order to find the right place, he carved a crane out of wood and it flew away and finally landed in the place where Songgwang-sa is today. There he built a small hermitage on Mount Chogye-san which he expanded to accommodate his growing community and it became known as Kilsang-sa and eventually Songgwang-sa. The Masters' Portrait Hall was built where the bird actually landed and the temple came to represent the Sangha, the followers of the Buddha.

Chinul exhorted his fellow meditators in the true spirit of the community he had founded in the following way:

"… we will renounce fame and profit and stay in seclusion in the mountain forests. There, we will form a community designed to foster constant training in concentration and wisdom. Through worship of the Buddha, recitation of texts, and even through common work, we will each discharge the duties which we are assigned and nourish the self-nature in all situations. We vow to pass our whole lives free from entanglements and to follow the higher pursuits of accomplished and true men. Wouldn't this be wonderful?"

Master Chinul was the Korean source of part of a great and ancient Buddhist debate which is still going on. He believed and taught that enlightenment is quite easily reached but that practice must continue afterwards in order that the person gets rid of the habit energies. This was called Sudden Awakening and Gradual Cultivation as opposed to Sudden Awakening and Sudden Cultivation, in which, after the struggle to reach the difficult stage of enlightenment, cultivation is no longer necessary.

View of the bridge (Songgwang-sa temple)

*Entrance
(Songgwang-sa temple)*

The Teaching Hall, the Masters' Portrait Hall and the residence of the Spiritual Leader are in the highest positions in Songgwang-sa because this is one of the Three Jewels Temples, making it different from other temples.

Songgwang-sa Temple was destroyed during the Hideyoshi Invasion and rebuilt sometime in the Choson Dynasty. Before destruction, Songgwang-sa Temple had grown to a large size, with many monks in residence. After the Hideyoshi Invasion, the temple was repaired and rebuilt many times but it never returned to its former glory. In 1988, however, the monk-in-charge worked hard to re-establish the former greatness of the temple by building it up according to the original foundations. Fourteen buildings were reconstructed including the magnificent Main Hall.

The Main Hall was built in 1988. Usually the Main Hall is the highest building but in Songgwang-sa that is not so. The Teaching Hall, the Masters' Portrait Hall and the residence of the Spiritual Leader are in the highest positions in Songgwang-sa because this is one of the Three Jewels Temples, making it different from other temples. In the Main Hall, the three main statues are the past Buddha, Dipankara, the present-day Buddha, Sakyamuni, and the Future Buddha, Maitreya. Along with the Buddhas, there are four Bodhisattvas: Manjusri, the Bodhisattva of Wisdom, Samantabhadra, the Bodhisattva of Practice, Avalokitesvara, the Bodhisattva of Compassion, and Ksitigarbha, the Bodhisattva who helps the suffering.

Just near the residence of the Spiritual Leader of Songgwang-sa is his assistant's living place. This little house dates from the 15th century and has a traditional

Roof Tile

chimney. It is one of the oldest living quarters still in use in Korea.

National Treasure No. 42 is kept at Songgwang-sa Temple. It is a wooden Buddha-triad casket, which seems to have been created using techniques foreign to Korea. Another National Treasure is No. 302: the building housing the Medicine Buddha, the Universal Healer, which was constructed without girders or beams. There is also one 800-year-old stump of an aromatic tree. Two bridges span a picturesque stream that flows in front of the temple entrance; the arch-covered one is considered architecturally unusual. In front of the main bridge-entrance into the temple, there are two small houses completely separate from the rest of the temple. Opinions vary on their purpose. Some say they were for keeping the name and remains of the dead who had specially asked to be kept near the temple for a period of regret after their death. Others say they were the place in which, after a bath, members of the royal family donned their wedding clothes just before marriage. These houses are unique to Songgwang-sa.

The late Master Kusan (1901-1983) set up an International Zen Center at Songgwang-sa Temple. Many foreigners who wished to experience life in a Zen Temple were attracted to this beautiful place; today, people still come from all over the world to live and practice here.

Sonam-sa, a temple on the other side of Chogye-san Mountain, is well worth a visit, too.

In front of the main bridge-entrance into the temple, there are two small houses completely separate from the rest of the temple.

Other Famous Temples

The Temple of Beautiful Gates: Pomo-sa

Pomo-sa stands on Kumjong-san, a mountain at the end of the T'aebaek Range which forms the backbone of the Korean peninsula. The mountain is carefully described in a Choson Dynasty geography book as having a huge rock at the summit on top of which there is a golden well which never, ever dries up. Legend tells that the water of this well has very special magical properties. One day a golden fish came from heaven and has lived there ever since. Thus the name of the temple came to be "Heavenly

7-tier Pagoda(Pomo-sa temple)

The One-pillac Gate(Pomo-sa temple)

Fish." Elsewhere it is said that the fish came from Nirvana, the Buddhist state of non-suffering. So the temples name became "Where fish from Nirvana Play."

It is recorded that Pomo-sa Temple was established by Master Uisang (625-702) in 678 during the reign of King Munmu (r. 661-681), one of the greatest Shilla kings, the first to unite the peninsula in 668. During one of the Japanese invasions of the peninsula, the king had a dream in which he was told to get Master Uisang to chant for seven days and then establish a temple on Kumjong-san Mountain. So the king organized the meeting and, at the end, the earth opened up and all the Buddhas and Bodhisattvas appeared and helped to drive away the Japanese.

Destroyed during the Hideyoshi Invasion, Pomo-sa Temple was reconstructed in 1602 and renovated in 1613. However, Shilla pagodas and lanterns still remain.

Pomo-sa is very famous for its gates. The temple is laid out in an unusual manner. The compound, composed of three levels, is clearly divided. The upper level is around the Main Hall. The second level is around the Poje-ru, the "Save all Beings" Hall and the lower part includes the three gates. The first gate is called the One-pillar Gate. It was built in 1614 and is Provincial Treasure No. 12. One reason for the strange name is that, when you look from one side, the two pillars appear as one! Another is that all who enter

Pomo-sa is very famous for its gates. The temple is laid out in an unusual manner. The compound, composed of three levels, is clearly divided. The upper level is around the Main Hall. The second level is around the Poje-ru, the "Save all Beings" Hall and the lower part includes the three gates.

are urged to search for the truth of the oneness of mind. The second gate is the Four Guardians' Gate where the four awesome protectors of the temple greet you. The Four Guardians all bear a fierce countenance and trample the opponents of Buddhism under their feet. Of Hindu origin these protectors are said to have helped Siddhartha Gautama, the Buddha-to-be, to leave his father's house on the night of his renunciation by each taking hold of one

hoof of Siddhartha's horse and lifting him over the palace walls.

The third gate, Gate of Non-duality represents the fact that, though the visitor is passing from the secular world into the spiritual world of the temple, these two worlds are not different from one another, they are not-two, non-dual.

The third level of the compound centers around the very beautiful Main Hall. It is Treasure No. 434 and was rebuilt by Master Myojun in 1614. The interior wooden carvings show a very refined level of Choson Dynasty craftsmanship. On the ceiling, there are many flowers which have been carved because of the legend that, whenever the Buddha teaches, flowers always fall from the heavens.

Pomo-sa has two main stupas. The three-storey stupa is from the Shilla Period about 830. It is four meters in height and is Treasure No. 250. The seven-storey stupa is new. Relics of the Buddha, brought to Korea by a Indian monk, have been enshrined within it. Just nearby there is the only stone lantern in Pomo-sa, Pusan Cultural Asset No. 16 which dates from the 9th century.

There is a famous painting of Vairocana in Pomo-sa. It used to hang behind the statue but now it is in a separate building. The harmony of colors gives the viewer a lovely feeling when looking at the painting.

In the mountains near Pomo-sa Temple, there are 11 different hermitages. Each one is very individual and delightful to visit. Pomo-sa is a wonderful temple to go to because, as you climb up above sprawling Pusan, you can enjoy the famous forest of wisteria trees.

The Main Hall
(Chondung-sa temple,
Treasure No. 178)

A Temple of Emotions: Chondung-sa

Well known as the sanctuary to which Korean kings with their courts fled to take refuge from the numerous Mongol and Manchurian invasions which took place during the Koryo and Choson dynasties.

This is a temple which tells the story of sweet revenge. What has revenge got to do with a Buddhist temple? One would think little as people who know anything about Buddhism, think of compassion and Buddhism in one breath.

Chondung-sa is a temple on Kanghwa Island to the west of Seoul, at the mouth of the Han River. Well known as the sanctuary to which Korean kings with their courts fled to take refuge from the numerous Mongol and Manchurian invasions which took place during the Koryo and Choson dynasties, King Kojong (r. 1213-1259) moved the capital to the island in 1232 in order to be safe from invaders.

The main fortress, Samnang-song, which houses the temple, Chondung-sa, dates from the time of the 25th Koryo king, Ch'ungyol (r. 1204-1308). The king had two wives. The first wife was Chinese, a daughter of Kublai Khan. The second was Korean Queen Chonghwa. Queen Chonghwa was jealous of the favor shown to her Chinese counterpart and so obtained a potion from a soothsayer.

The rumor of her actions passed around the court and she was imprisoned. In her loneliness she was drawn to the temple, then known as Chinjong-sa. She offered a beautiful jade lamp to the temple in 1282 from which the name "Temple of the Donated or Inherited Lamp" or Chondung-sa came.

The site of present-day Chondung-sa is ancient. The first temple was built in 381 CE by a Buddhist monk. The site must have been considered auspicious and important as the first buildings went up only nine years after the introduction of Buddhism to the Koguryo Kingdom in 372. After that the temple was burnt down and reconstructed many times.

Chondung-sa's present-day Main Hall dates back to 1855 and is a reconstruction of a hall which was completed in 1621 following the destruction of an earlier one by fire in 1614. It is a shrine to Sakyamuni Buddha who is depicted in the style of Sokkur-am — the famous grotto in Kyongju (see Sokkur-am). The Buddha is flanked on the left by Manjusri, the Bodhisattva of Perfect Wisdom, and on the right by Samantabhadra, the Bodhisattva of Perfect Compassionate Action.

As you approach the hall, look carefully way up in the eaves at the corners of the rafters of the hipped-and-gabled roof, there you can just see a tiny human figure, one at each corner. The story goes something like this:

When the hall was being built, a special carpenter was hired. He stayed in the nearby village next to the liquor shop. There he fell in love with the daughter of the owner of the shop but, as he was poor, he could only promise to marry the girl when the hall was completed. Eventually the carpenter was paid and he set off to claim his bride. The girl had other plans. She took the money and ran away with her other love. And so the forsaken carpenter carved his two-timing girl up in

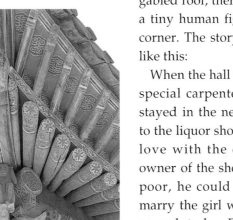
The edge of the eaves (Chondung-sa temple)

> She offered a beautiful jade lamp to the temple in 1282 from which the name "Temple of the Donated or Inherited Lamp" or Chondung-sa came.

the rafters eternally bearing the burden of her deceitfulness.

Revenge at Chondung-sa does not stop there. Just near the entrance, there's a huge ginkgo tree. The tree was famous for the great yield which it gave every year and so sometime during the Japanese Colonial Period (1910-1945), the oppressors demanded more ginkgo nuts than ever before. At this Master Chusong, a monk renowned for his special powers, became annoyed. For three days he chanted under the tree and from that day to this not a single nut has fallen.

After the Main Hall, the next most important object to see is the iron bell, Treasure No. 393, which is housed in a small building near the entrance. The inscription engraved on it says that it was cast at a Chinese temple, Chungming-su, in Hwaichow, China in 1097, during the Northern Sung Period; it is the only Chinese bell designated a Korean treasure.

Another of Chondung-sa's claims to fame is the fact that it was here that the z81,258 wooden printing blocks that make up the famous Tripitaka Koreana (now preserved in Haein-sa Temple) were carved and stored; there are still 104 wood-blocks kept at Chondung-sa ? one was lost during the war. They are kept in the Main Hall to the right of the Buddha.

There are three more important shrines at Chondung-sa. A Medicine Buddha Hall next to the Main Hall; a small building housing some of the traditional gods; and a shrine to the Bodhisattva who helps people who are in trouble. In order to reach Chondung-sa, you have to pass through the entrance to Samnang-song Fortress. The fortress is said to have been built in a single day by the three sons of the mythical founder of Korea, T'angun, who was born in 2333 BCE. He was the son of a bear woman and Hwanung, a heavenly god.

The fortress is said to have been built in a single day by the three sons of the mythical founder of Korea, T'angun, who was born in 2333 BCE. He was the son of a bear woman and Hwanung, a heavenly god.

Entrance(Yongju-sa temple)

The Temple of Filial Piety: Yongju-sa

Yongju-sa is the result of a son's longing for his dead father and a tribute to filial piety. The father of King Chongjo (r. 1776-1800) died and he could not rid his mind of the image of the death scene. Some time passed and then, one day, he heard a lecture on the Parental

The Main Hall(Yongju-sa temple)

Yongju-sa is the result of a son's longing for his dead father and a tribute to filial piety. The father of King Chongjo (r. 1776-1800) died and he could not rid his mind of the image of the death scene.

Benevolence Sutra, a text which explains the debt that children have to their parents. He decided to rebuild Kilyang-sa in memory of his father and move his father's tomb there. Throughout his life, he visited the temple often.

One day when the king was there, he noticed that the pine trees near his father's tomb were dying from being eaten by a kind of caterpillar. He was so upset that the pine trees near the tomb should die that he took one of the caterpillars and killed it by biting into it with his teeth. After that there were no more caterpillars eating the trees.

Originally the temple had been constructed by Master Yomgu in 854 and then greatly enlarged in 952. Even though the temple is not in the mountains, far away from the bustle of the world, it bestows a sense of peace and well-being on those who enter its gates.

The name of the temple, as is so often the case, comes from a legend. On the night before the day of the completion of the building activities, King Chongjo dreamt of a dragon soaring up into the sky and there receiving the Pearl of Truth, the Wish-fulfilling Gem. (This is the ball-like structure that most dragons carry in their mouth.) Therefore the temple came to be called "Dragon's Pearl of Truth Temple."

Dragons are auspicious animals with divine properties. Considered a symbol of regal authority, the dragon was

The Main Hall enshrines three Buddha (Yongju-sa temple)

also thought to dispel evil spirits. Dragons are usually related to heaven and water and are used in rain rituals. Considered protectors, they have always been seen as important in preserving Korea from invasion and so there are many legends about sea dragons who defend the peninsula. King Munmu wished to be reborn as a great dragon to protect his country and so he was buried under a large rock in the sea off the east coast. The kings of the family who founded the Koryo Dynasty were all reputed to be descendants of the Divine Sea Dragon and each one of the family had a dragon scale in his or her armpit.

The temple soon became a major one and in 1911 was made one of the 24 main temples of the Korean Buddhist Chogye Order; it has 48 smaller temples under it in that area. The monks' training school was established in 1955. The meditation center was built in 1969 and has become the main one of Kangwon Province.

Yongju-sa is unusual in many respects. The gates are patterned after the royal ancestors' shrine or even a palace and not after a normal temple.

Yongju-sa is unusual in many respects. The gates are patterned after the royal ancestors' shrine or even a palace and not after a normal temple. Thus Sammungak, Three Gates, stands where the Four Guardians' Gate should stand as in the Pulmyo, one of the famous royal shrines. Next there is a five-storey stupa in front of a pavilion and not in front of a Main Hall; this is another example of the temple being like a palace. Again as in a palace, the pillars are made of stone not of wood and some of the buildings are in palace style.

The Main Hall enshrines three Buddhas. Sakyamuni, the Historical Buddha, is in the center, the Medicine Buddha is to the east and Amitabha, the Buddha of the Western Paradise, is to the west. Behind the statues is the only western-style picture in a temple in Korea. It is painted in perspective which is very unusual. The canopy over the

There are some
other important
artifacts at the
temple. Apart from
a golden incense
burner and a copper
incense burner
donated to the
temple by King
Chongjo, there are
two books written
by the king which
show his deep
feeling for
Buddhism and his
strong devotion to
his father.

statues is very delicately and finely carved. Below it are five dragons in the clouds with the sun and a phoenix. On either side there are celestial beings as well.

The copper bell of Yongju-sa, National Treasure No. 120, is very special. It is presumed to have been cast in the early 10th century, during the Koryo Dynasty, because of the style of the dragon. Shilla bells have a dragon holding the bell with two legs. In Yongju-sa, the dragon is holding the bell up with just one leg, important in the study of bells.

There are some other important artifacts at the temple. Apart from a golden incense burner and a copper incense burner donated to the temple by King Chongjo, there are two books written by the king which show his deep feeling for Buddhism and his strong devotion to his father. There is an unusual five-storey stupa behind the hall dedicated to Ksitigarbha, the Bodhisattva who helps those in trouble. It has a small wooden sign with the names of the donors on it. This stupa was also built for King Chongjo's father.

A Temple Overlooking a River: Shilluk-sa

The temple overlooks the wide Southern Han River. Sitting in the little traditional pavilion on the banks of the river, one can easily imagine terror provoked by the dragon-horse...

On either side of the Southern Han River the people were being tyrannized by a dragon-horse who lived on an island in the middle of the river. Master Naong (1320-1376) put a magical bridle over it and tamed the wild animal. Therefore the temple came to be called "Divine Bridle."

Apart from this legend, the founding of the temple seems shrouded in mystery.

One thing is certain, Master Naong definitely had a lot to do with this

Full View(Shilluk-sa temple)

*Chosa-dang
(Shilluk-sa temple,
Treasure No. 180)*

**Master Naong
lived most of his
life at Shilluk-sa.
At his death,
clouds of five
colors covered the
mountain and
there was rain
from a cloudless
sky falling on the
temple.**

temple. He was a remarkable man and his story is woven into almost every aspect of Shilluk-sa.

Master Naong was ordained at the age of 20 and spent ten years in China. He then became a celebrated Zen master who formed his own school of thought using very dynamic teaching methods and was also appointed "King's Teacher," a special position of great importance. He integrated chanting — for him a state of mind in which there is no thinking — into the dominant Meditation School and advocated never forgetting the name of Amitabha, the Buddha of the Western Paradise.

Master Naong lived most of his life at Shilluk-sa. At his death, clouds of five colors covered the mountain and there was rain from a cloudless sky falling on the temple. When the body was cremated, it yielded innumerable relics, these were enshrined in a special bell-shaped stupa — reminiscent of Indian ones — which is Treasure No. 228. Some time later, the temple was greatly enlarged.

The tomb of King Sejong (r. 1418-1450) was moved to Yoju in 1469 and it was decided that Shilluk-sa would become the royal memorial temple for the king and the royal family. The temple was greatly rebuilt in 1472 when about 200 rooms were repaired or newly made. The name was changed a number of times, eventually becoming Shilluk-sa. After that many Confucian scholars passed time at the temple — in spite of the persecution of Buddhism — until the 16th century Japanese and 17th century Mongolian invasions which left most of the temple in ruins. The final rebuilding was in 1928.

The Main Hall is Provincial Asset No. 132. It is a Paradise

The Main Hall is Provincial Asset No. 132. It is a Paradise Hall enshrining Amitabha Buddha, Samantabhadra, the Bodhisattva of Practice, and Avalokitesvara, the Bodhisattva of Compassion.

Hall enshrining Amitabha Buddha, Samantabhadra, the Bodhisattva of Practice, and Avalokitesvara, the Bodhisattva of Compassion. The calligraphy board which hangs there is the writing of Master Naong and it says "Hundreds of Millions of Years." The hall is beautifully decorated. On the left wall there is a painting of Ksitigarbha with entourage and on the back wall is an altar for death and memorial ceremonies. Above the table there is a picture of Ch'ilsong, the Seven Buddhas. One more picture shows the guardian of the Buddha's teachings, Tongjin. He is accompanied by gods, ministers and officials.

Originally, in the late 14th century, to the south of the Paradise Hall, there was a Tripitaka Hall, a place for housing the Buddhist texts in the form of wood-blocks. The monument there, Treasure No. 230, was written by a famous scholar. It records various facts about the shape and style of the building and the fact that the texts were carried to Haein-sa.

Especially beautiful is the Judgement Hall with Ksitigarbha and the Ten Judges. Attending the kings are various servants and behind them are the pictures of the various hells, with their tortures. From the Buddhist viewpoint, hell is not necessarily somewhere else, it is

Bell-shaped stupa
(Shilluk-sa temple, Treasure No. 228)

The Seven-story
brick pagoda
(Shilluk-sa temple.
Treasure No. 226).

here and now, often created in our own minds.

In the compound of the house where the head monk lives, there is a special trestle garden which dates from 1468. Also in the same compound there is a statue of Master Naong. Behind the statue there is a picture of the master with masters Muhak (1321-1405) and Chi-gong (?-1363). Muhak was advisor of Yi Tae-jo who founded of the Choson Dynasty and moved the capital to Seoul according to advice from Master Muhak who was a famous geomancer. (The name "Seoul" is derived from the place near which the Buddha spent much time, Sravasti. In Chinese, Sravasti became Sarbol and in Korean, Seoul.) Master Chi-gong was an Indian monk whose Sanskrit name was Dhyanabhadra. Tibetan monks believe that he is an incarnation of a Tibetan lama. He came to Korea in 1328. After his death in China, his remains were brought back to Korea.

Other remembrances of Master Naong include a marvelous ginkgo tree planted by the master at the foot of the hill. Also the master's meditation place by the Southern Han River is marked by a pavilion next to a little pagoda.

To the east of the monastery is a hill on which is a seven-storey, brick pagoda which is 9.4 meters high and is the only existing Koryo brick pagoda. It was erected in honor of the famous monk Wonhyo who visited Shilluk-sa. The base is granite and the rest is brick with various impressed floral decorations.

The Home of Manjusri Bodhisattva: Woljong-sa

Shilla Master Chajang founded this temple, Calm Moon, on Odae-san, a famous mountain in Korea. It was destined to become a famous place for spreading Buddhism. The story of the origin of the temple goes something like this...

Master Chajang went to China in about 636 because he had a great wish to see Manjusri Bodhisattva on Wutai-shan, the name of a mountain which, when pronounced in Korean, becomes Odae-san. Following the Chinese system there are five plateaux on Odae-san Mountain, part of the

Master Chajang chanted before a stone statue of the Bodhisattva beside a pond, hoping to fulfill his long-cherished wish.

T'aebaek Mountain Range on which the principle Bodhisattvas live. Each abode is marked with a hermitage. In the middle there is Saja-am, to the east is Kwanum-am, to the west is Sujong-am, to the south is Chijang-am, and to the north is Miruk-am. There is a story that the two sons of King Chongshin, Poch'on and Hyomyong, each met 50,000 Bodhisattvas on the five peaks. Therefore this place is considered very special.

It is said that on this mountain, Master Chajang chanted before a stone statue of the Bodhisattva beside a pond, hoping to fulfill his long-cherished wish. On the seventh night of his religious practice he had a dream in which the Buddha gave him a poem of four lines. After waking up, he couldn't understand the words because they were in Sanskrit. Next day, a monk came and gave him a robe of the Buddha's, one of the Buddha's bowls and one piece of the Buddha's skull. The monk then remarked that the master looked pale and troubled. Master Chajang explained that he had received a verse he could not understand. The monk explained the verse thus,

"Thoroughly to understand all teachings of the Buddha;
Selfhood possesses nothing;
Understand the teachings in this way;
Then you can see Rochana Buddha."

The octagonal nine-story pagoda (Woljong-sa temple, Nat'l Treasure No. 48)

*Bodhisattva
(Woljong-sa temple,
Treasure No. 139)*

The mysterious monk then told the master to go to Odae-san in Shilla and that there he would find 10,000 Manjusris.

After seven more days of chanting, a dragon appeared who told him that the old monk had been Manjusri and that now he must go and build a temple to the Bodhisattva. So he set off for Shilla.

In 643, Chajang reached Odae-san but the mountain was so veiled in fog that he couldn't see anything. During the three days that he waited he stayed in a thatched hut - this hut became Woljong-sa much later. The master left and went to Wonyung-sa where he finally met Manjusri and recognized the Bodhisattva.

The Main Hall, according to its name, should enshrine a Vairocana Buddha.

Various masters stayed here for different lengths of time until finally a temple was built. Burnt down and rebuilt a number of times, the last disaster was during the Korean War when about ten buildings were burnt down by the Korean army - many temples had become refuges for the rebel forces and so they were destroyed.

The Main Hall, according to its name, should enshrine a Vairocana Buddha. Instead there is a statue of Sakyamuni but the more important statue is of an unusual Bodhisattva, 1.8 meters high, probably a Medicine Bodhisattva, National Treasure No. 139. Said to have been found in the Diamond Pond to the south of the temple, the statue is offering something. The story of this Bodhisattva originates from the Lotus Sutra. The head is covered with a hat, the face is long and the ears are slightly hidden by long hair. Around the neck there are three lines which are so beautifully carved that they look like necklaces. The elbow is resting on the head of a young boy. Because of its unusual style, the statue is thought to have been carved in the 11th century by craftsmen belonging to a special sect; it is therefore important to the history of carving.

The octagonal nine-storey pagoda is National Treasure No. 48. It stands 15.2 meters high and because of its harmony and the skill of the carving, it is representative of many-angled, many-storied stupas of the Koryo Period.

One of the more recent masters, Han-am (1876-1951), lived here. When he was a 22, while on a journey to the Diamond Mountains (traditionally very important to Buddhists, now in North Korea), he suddenly got the strong impression that he should become a monk. So he ordained immediately and lived most of his life at Woljong-sa.

During the Korean war, when the Korean army was sent, he saved part of the temple. As the soldiers came to execute their orders to destroy the temple, the master put on his ceremonial monk's robes and went into one of the halls. The solders ordered him to come out but he replied, "You are soldiers, you have to follow orders, it is your duty. I am a monk, so my duty is to keep this hall, so please burn it and go." The soldiers couldn't bring themselves to destroy it, so they only burnt one door. The master then returned to the hermitage where he stayed. On his way there he stuck his stick in the ground and it has since grown into a fine tree, a maple.

The Temple of Compassion: Naksan-sa

Nak-san is Korea's Potalaka Mountain, the place where Avalokitesvara Bodhisattva lives. Since ancient times the subject of much respect, the Bodhisattva embodies the idea of perfect compassion. Many miraculous stories are told and many special ceremonies and art works relating to Avalokitesvara have made the Bodhisattva into a very central figure in Mahayana Buddhism.

The Bodhisattva is depicted in many different forms. Sometimes with four, six or more hands, there are many statues and paintings in which Avalokitesvara has 1,000 hands, each with an

Wontong bojon(Naksan-sa temple)

Hongryon-am
(Naksan-sa temple)

eye, so that the Bodhisattva can see where those in trouble are and help them. Avalokitesvara represents the ultimate in compassion within each one of us and is usually considered to be neither male nor female. The Bodhisattva lives on a sea-bound island. The sea is filled with protecting dragons to whom all but the pure of heart fall prey. In the background of many paintings are waterfalls, rocks and often luscious plants and trees.

It is therefore no surprise to find Korea' s Potalaka on Nak-san Mountain overlooking the Eastern Sea. The temple built there is called Naksan-sa.

It is therefore no surprise to find Korea' s Potalaka on Nak-san Mountain overlooking the Eastern Sea. The temple built there is called Naksan-sa. It was founded by Master Uisang in 676 CE, the 16th year of the reign of King Munmu. The temple is dominated by a statue of Avalokitesvara which took six years to create. It recalls the legend of the founding of the temple...

The master, a famous Avatamsa monk, heard that Avalokitesvara was staying in a cave on a mountain overlooking the Eastern Sea. So he went there to meet the Bodhisattva. After seven days of spiritual practice, he received a magical string of Buddhist beads made of pure crystal. Next the dragon of the Eastern Sea gave him a fabulous jewel. The master then practiced for a further seven days and only then met Avalokitesvara and was told, "On the peak above my seat, you will find a pair of bamboo plants growing. Build a Main Hall there." After building the hall the master deposited the beads and the jewel inside.

This is the central theme of the Avatamsaka School which Uisang spread throughout Korea on his return from China.

Soon after, Uisang's friend, Wonhyo, came to visit. On his way he is supposed to have met two different women, both were forms of the Bodhisattva. When he reached the cave, a storm suddenly rose up and he was unable to enter and meet the true Bodhisattva. During Master Wonhyo's visit, the two friends discussed a poem written in the form of a seal. This seal, the Avatamsa Ilsung popkye to – literally "Decorated by flowers, One Vehicle, Reality of Myself in the World Seal" – which is in the shape of the mathematical diagram for infinity, was written by Uisang as a present for his teacher, Chih-yen, in China when he was leaving after studying there for eight years. It is one of the great offerings of the Korean people to the world and its essence is:

In one is all,
In all is one.
One is identical to all,
All is identical to one.

Flower Walls of Nakan-sa temple

Hong-ye Gate(Naksan-sa temple)

The fine seven-storey pagoda, Treasure No. 499, is also believed to have been erected during the reign of King Sejo.

This is the central theme of the Avatamsaka School which Uisang spread throughout Korea on his return from China.

During the Choson Dynasty, the temple was repeatedly rebuilt and destroyed. The present buildings date from 1953.

The Main Hall is a splendid tribute to Avalokitesvara. Exquisitely decorated, the hall is full of statues of the Bodhisattva in various poses. There you can see the many forms that Avalokitesvara takes and appreciate the skill of Korean wood carving.

In spite of the many destructions and reconstructions, a few ancients things remain. The Arched Gate (Provincial Tangible Cultural Property No. 33), built in 1467 during the reign of King Sejo (1455-68), is believed to have been built from 26 stones each of which was contributed by each one of the 26 magistrates governing the 26 towns of the area by order of the king.

The fine seven-storey pagoda, Treasure No. 499, is also believed to have been erected during the reign of King Sejo. It measures 6.2 meters high, including the finial. The body and roof stone of each storey is made of a single stone. It is well preserved, especially in that it has an intact finial which consists of an inverted bowl, a wheel and a bijou on a bronze staff, resembling those of Tibetan style pagodas found in Yuan, China. Another Provincial Tangible Cultural Property, No. 34, is the adobe wall surrounding the Main Hall. It also dates from the reign of King Sejo and is highly regarded for the designs which have been used in its creation. Only part of it is original, the rest has been recently restored.

The bronze bell is dated 1469 according to an inscription. The Bodhisattvas, the pattern of lotus petals and waves on the body of the bell and the twin dragons on the top have all been beautifully cast.

Naksan-sa has not forgotten Avalokitesvara's home. Potalaka is represented by a lovely two-storied hall. Nearby is a pond full of water-lilies - at the right time of year.

The Temple of Frequent Change: Shinhung-sa

Shinhung-sa is the main temple of the area known as Outer Sorak-san Mountain. The temple is remarkable for its constant changing over the centuries. For not only did it change position and name, but also the school of Buddhism to which it adhered.

It was founded by Master Chajang in 652 and named Hyangsong-sa.

Actually Shinhung-sa stood where the New Sorak Hotel stands today. It was founded by Master Chajang in 652 and named Hyangsong-sa. The temple was burned down in 699 and Master Uisang rebuilt the temple three years later on its present site.

Once more destroyed in 1645 at the time of the Japanese invasions, all the monks left the temple and only three monks remained. One night the three monks had a dream in which they met a god who told them what to do. He said that if they built the temple behind the original site, then the temple would never be touched by three main disasters: fire, water and wind. The monks built the temple there and called it Shinhung-sa, "Divinely Inspired Temple." There is a one kilometer path leading up to the One-pillar Gate. The path passes relic containers and memorial tablets of great monks who have lived and died at the temple.

*The Main Hall
(Paradise Hall, Shinhung-sa temple)*

Next comes the main compound. Behind the Gate of the Four Guardians there is a two-storey study hall. On the stone stairway and retaining wall near the Main Hall there are several unusual reliefs. These are guardians, defending Buddhism from those that would harm it. The temple is built on a foundation of natural stone with four large natural stones at the corners of the base. The Main Hall, a Paradise Hall, is built on an east-west axis

facing towards the east. On the walls of the outside of the building there are the Ten Oxherding pictures and some pictures of stories about famous Zen masters. Inside the hall, Amitabha is enshrined accompanied by Avalokitesvara and Mahastramprapta, the Bodhisattva of Power. The statues are said to have been made in the time of Uisang, in the 7th century. They sit under a bright canopy of yellow dragons and behind the statues is a painting showing Sakyamuni with various Bodhisattvas, the guardians at the four corners and some monks including a very aged Kasyapa and a very young-looking Ananda, the Buddha's long term attendant. On the northern wall is a painting of the protector of Dharma, Tongjin, with celestial beings, ministers, Bodhisattvas, and gods. Included in the gods is the Kitchen God who has an unusual beard and holds antlers in his hand. There are also warriors armed with swords, tridents and other weapons.

The Ten Oxherding pictures, dating from 12th century Song China (1126-1279), are very important to the school of Zen. Although the style and actual pictures vary enormously, the message of the pictures remains the same (see p. 149).

To the right of the Main Hall there is the Bell Pavilion which is a very good example of Choson architecture.

To the right of the Main Hall there is the Bell Pavilion which is a very good example of Choson architecture. The Judgement Hall is dedicated to the benevolent Ksitigarbha, the Bodhisattva who cares for those in trouble. Behind the statue is a painting showing the Bodhisattva and guardians. The walls and ceiling are painted with Taoistic images.

Recently, during restoration, some interesting printing plates made of wood were found. They are thought to date from the 17th century and they contain some texts, like the Lotus Sutra, some Buddhist ceremonies and the writings of some Korean masters.

The Sanshin between the Main Hall and the Judgement Hall contains a picture of the Mountain God with his tiger. Usually pictured with a tiger, Sanshin is particularly remembered after any large ceremony. This is because everyone is grateful for being able to have the temple built on the mountain. Toksong, the Lonely Hermit, is actually more Buddhist in origin and represents the sole practitioner. Ch'ilsong, the Big Dipper, controls human life expectancy and women who have just given birth traditionally offered a skein of thread to Ch'ilsong as a symbol of their hope for a long life for their baby. In Shinhung-sa, Ch'ilsong is surrounded by the sun and the moon, seven stars, the master of the South Polar star, and lots of heavenly beings.

Two kilometers from the temple there is a lovely pagoda, Treasure No. 443. In the surrounding mountains and forests there are a number of interesting hermitages, some of which partly date back to the time of Master Chajang.

> **Pulguk-sa Temple epitomizes the spirit of Shilla, bearing witness to the great architectural achievements of that period and showing a highly refined form of aesthetic beauty.**

The Temple of the Two Pagodas: Pulguk-sa

Pulguk-sa is the best known and, if we accept the legends, one of the oldest temples in Korea. The name means "Buddha Land" and it is located on the outskirts of Kyongju, the capital of the Unified Shilla Period. The temple, first built in 535 during the reign of King Pophung (r. 514-540), was much smaller than the present structure. King Pophung was the first Shilla king to accept Buddhism. He and his queen eventually renounced the throne and were ordained.

In 751, the temple was built up during the reign of King

Pulguk-sa temple

Kyongdok (r. 742-765) by Kim Tae-song, the chief minister, in honor of his parents. There is a story that Kim Tae-song's birth into the prime minister's family was announced by a mysterious voice. To honor his parents, he designed and had Pulguk-sa Temple built. He recalled the poor parents of his previous birth, too, and built Sokkuram in their memory.

Pulguk-sa Temple epitomizes the spirit of Shilla, bearing witness to the great architectural achievements of

Pulguk-sa Temple
(Blue and White Cloud Bridge,
Nat'l Treasure No. 22, 23)

*Sakyamuni pagoda
(Pulguk-sa temple, Nat'l Treasure No. 21)*

*Pagoda of Many Treasures
(Pulguk-sa temple, Nat'l Treasure
No. 20)*

Legend tells that they were both created by a mason called Asadal who came from the former kingdom of Paekje.

that period and showing a highly refined form of aesthetic beauty. Twenty-three times renovated – the most recent was in 1973 – the symmetry, balance and grace of former times is ever preserved. The temple is built on a series of terraces made of gigantic stones fitted together without mortar.

There are six national treasures to be seen. The most important are probably two of the most famous monuments in the whole of Korea. They are the two mortarless stone pagodas which stand complementing each other in the courtyard of the temple. Sakyamuni Pagoda, National Treasure No. 21, symbolizing the Buddha's contemplation and detachment, is representative of the trend in the Unified Shilla Period when pagodas were simplified to consist of three storeys. The ratio of the widths is 4:3:2, the width of the lower base being equal to the height of the main structure above the upper base. The simplicity of this pagoda is enhanced by the complexity of its twin, Pagoda of Many Treasures, National Treasure No. 20. It is actually an enlarged relic holder, one of the types of vessels used to store the remains of the Buddha and, later, other great monks.

Legend tells that they were both created by a mason called Asadal who came from the former kingdom of Paekje. He left his young wife Asanyo promising to return

Pulguk-sa Temple is particularly famous for the graceful staircases, actually bridges, leading up to the temple complex.

as soon as the pagodas were completed. After years of waiting, Asanyo journeyed to Kyongju but was prohibited from visiting the pagodas as no outsiders were allowed. She was told to wait near a pond and that, when the pagodas were completed, they would be reflected in the pond. She waited long and patiently and eventually, out of desperation, cast herself into the pond; Sakyamuni Pagoda is sometimes called "Pagoda without Refection."

Pulguk-sa Temple is particularly famous for the graceful staircases, actually bridges, leading up to the temple complex. They are the oldest stone bridges in Korea and are called bridges because they lead from the secular world to the Land of the Buddha. In addition, originally there was a lake in front of the temple and boats used to float visitors to these staircases. The one to the east is called Blue and White Cloud Bridge (National Treasure No. 23). The second bridge-stairway, to the west, is called the Lotus Flower and the Seven Gems (National Treasure No. 22).

There are two, 8th century, bronze statues, one of Amitabha, the Buddha of Light (National Treasure No. 27), the other of Vairocana, the Buddha of Cosmic Power, (National Treasure No. 26). Both are believed to have been cast in the 8th century. The Amitabha statue is in the Paradise Hall which is connected to the Vairocana Hall by

northern India over 2,500 years ago, he was challenged as to his right to sit on the earth. He touched the ground and the earth bore witness to his many good deeds, granting him that right. The whole pose of the Buddha portrays the peace, tolerance and uprightness which Buddhism is famous for.

During the Choson Dynasty, when Buddhism was persecuted, this national masterpiece was forgotten. Then one cloudy day, in 1909, a lone postman suddenly had to take shelter from a thunderstorm. He dashed into the only place available: a cave. There, as his eyes grew accustomed to the dim light, he saw the magnificent statue.

The Lovely Avalokitesvara(Sokkur-am)

In 1913, the Japanese occupation government spent two years repairing the grotto. As cement was used, repairs had to be made again in 1920, and UNESCO further aided the government from 1961 to 1964 in further restoring the precious cave. It is now on the UNESCO Heritage list as one of the wonders of the world.

The Buddha has sat here for over 1,000 years. Unfor-tunately, in modern times, it has become necessary to protect the statue from vandals and from temperature changes. Therefore visitors can no longer enter the grotto itself. In spite of this, a visit to Sokkur-am Grotto is well worth the trip because the gaze of the Buddha will stay with you forever.

He found it on Mt. Ponhwang-san but the villagers refused to vacate the chosen spot. Once again, the dragon appeared. Threatening to hurl a massive rock on the village, the people fled and the dragon came crashing to the earth and exhaled its last breath. This is the site of the Main Hall of Pusok-sa today. To the west you can see a piece of rock, a small portion of the one hurled by the dragon. Therefore Pusok-sa is called "Temple of the Floating Stone." Uisang averted another Chinese invasion by performing a special ceremony some years later.

From a geomancy point of view, Pusok-sa is very auspicious. In Korean, as in Chinese, geomancy is called the study of "wind and water." The ideal site should be encircled by mountains with specially high ridges on the northern side extending to the east. These ridges are known as the Blue Dragon. On the western side there should be some more ridges and these are know as the White Tiger. In addition, Pusok-sa, constructed in 676 at the orders of King Munmu, is a temple which shows the transition period between those originally built in the plains during the period of the Three Kingdoms and those built in the mountains during the Koryo and Choson periods. The original temples were centered around a single pagoda—single Main Hall pattern. The later temples consisted of a Main Hall and two pagodas.

From the beginning Uisang made the temple the headquarters of his Avatamsaka sect. However, Korean Buddhism is never quite so clear-cut. The temple also has all the trappings of one dedicated to Pure Land, to the philosophy of the Western Paradise presided over by Amitabha Buddha.

Therefore the Main Hall, National Treasure No. 18, enshrines Amitabha. Originally built in 676, the present structure dates from 1358, one of the oldest wooden buildings in Korea. The architectural style is worth looking at closely. The foundation is of granite. The columns supporting the roof are fitted with brackets which seem complicated at first but which are actually amazingly simple. The hipped-and-gabled roof is in perfect proportion to the body of the building, giving the hall a unique feeling. Inside, the statue sits in the west facing east because it is an Amitabha, Buddha of the Western Paradise. It is the oldest clay statue in Korea,

Stone Lantern(Pusok-sa temple, Nat'l Treasure No. 17)

A masterpiece of
proportion and
design, the fine
reliefs of lotus
petals and
Bodhisattvas make
it a precious gem.

National Treasure No. 45, and, although it is a Koryo statue, it reflects faithfully the style of Shilla statues.

To the left of the Main Hall, at the bottom of a steep bluff, lies the legendary floating stone. To the right of the stone is a three-storey pagoda behind which is a pavilion dedicated to the Chinese girl who, in the form of a dragon, helped Master Uisang. The portrait in the pavilion is of the same girl.

Chosadang, National Treasure No. 19, a hall for keeping the portraits of great masters, lies 100 meters to the northeast of the Main Hall. It was built 150 years after the Main Hall. Originally, the building was decorated with wall paintings but these have been moved to a protected place. The six frescoes, four of guardians and two of Bodhisattvas, are National Treasure No. 46 and they are the best existing examples of Koryo Period wall painting.

Just under the eaves of Chosadang, there is a tree. It sprang from a stick which Uisang put there on his way to India. He is reputed to have foretold that if a tree grew it would never die. And so it is, ever green and blooming after 1,300 years!

Pusok-sa has many treasures. The flagpole supports are Treasure No. 255; the Koryo wood-blocks are Treasure No. 735; the pudo, conical stone objects in which the remains of famous monks are kept; the two stone pagodas; and the monument to Master Wonyung, a National Teacher of the Koryo Period, are only some of the wonderful objects which have survived Korea's turbulent history. In particular, the stone lantern, National Treasure No. 17 which dates from the Unified Shilla Period, should be carefully looked at. A masterpiece of proportion and design, the fine reliefs of lotus petals and Bodhisattvas make it a precious gem.

The Temple of the Future Buddha: Kumsan-sa

Master Chinp' yo decided to build a temple to Maitreya and call it Kumsan-sa.

Kumsan-sa or Gold Mountain Temple is located on Mt. Moak-san near Chonju.

Originally built in 600 CE, according to the temple records 38 monks were ordained at the temple in that same year. After numerous destructions and rebuildings, the present buildings were erected in 1635 after the others were destroyed in the Hideyoshi Invasion of the 16th century. There are many treasures which pre-date the present buildings. The temple is now one of the principle centers of the region and one of the biggest in Korea.

Master Chinp' yo (known around 742-780) was responsible for the construction of the temple from 762 to 766 when he enlarged the existing number of buildings. According to a legend, Master Chinp' yo, after returning from China, had a vision of Maitreya Buddha and he

Maitreya Buddha Hall
(Kumsan-sa temple, Nat'l Treasure No. 62)

Maitreya Buddha
(Kumsan-sa temple)

This Maitreya
Buddha Hall
(National Treasure
No. 62) is over 20
meters high. It is the
only ancient,
wooden, three-
storey hall in Korea,
each storey has a
different name and
so a different name
board.

received a book on divination in two rolls and 189 divination sticks from Maitreya. This book on divination then became the principal authority on the subject in Korea. And due to this, King Kyongdok invited the master to his palace in order to receive instruction and predictions.

Master Chinp' yo decided to build a temple to Maitreya and call it Kumsan-sa. On his way, he met a dragon king who presented the master with a robe of jade and guided him to Kum-san forest. There, miraculously, men and women from everywhere came to help. The temple was built in a few days and when it was completed, Maitreya came to give Chinp' yo his final ordination. In memory of this event, Chinp' yo created a Maitreya Buddha Hall, the focal point of Kumsan-sa. After that, the master set up a platform and taught the people well.

This Maitreya Buddha Hall (National Treasure No. 62) is over 20 meters high. It is the only ancient, wooden, three-storey hall in Korea, each storey has a different name and so a different name board. The first floor is "Great Compassion Hall." The second is "Dragon Flower Meeting" and the third is "Maitreya Hall." In order to support the immense roof, special corner eave pillars were created.

Enshrined is a statue of the future Buddha, Maitreya. This gilded, standing statue is 11.82 meters high and is flanked by two attendants, each 8.79 meters high. The Maitreya statue is modeled after a Shilla statue although it actually dates from the early 20th century. The hand position is one of "have no fear." The assistants date from the Choson Period. On the southern wall is a painting of Maitreya giving the monks' rules to Chinp' yo. Because of this strong connection with Maitreya, Kumsan-sa followed the Dharmalaksana, or Dharma Aspect School.

In Korea, the traditional buildings of palaces and temples are painted with amazingly bright colored geometrical patterns. These designs are called "tanch' ong," meaning "red and blue," the principle colors used. Tanch' ong was introduced to the peninsula through the Koguryo Kingdom probably somewhere about the time that Buddhism was accepted, in 372 CE. The main aim of tanch' ong is protection of the wood. The wood is carefully treated before applying the base or background pigment in order to protect it from humidity and decay. Then the design to be painted on is outlined using chalk powder over pinholes made in the paper of the design. Now the wood is ready to receive the bright colors of the mineral paints used. Finally a coating of oil is applied and the paintings are gone over with a hot iron. In this way the wood is protected from the elements as well as from mold and bugs.

In front of the Maitreya Hall is a strange hexagonal stone pagoda, Treasure No. 27. Dating from the Koryo Period, probably late 10th century, this kind of hexagonal, sometimes octagonal, pagoda was popular at the time. It stands 2.18 meters high and the 11 remaining storeys are well balanced. Originally it probably had 13 storeys.

Kumsan-sa Temple has many

> In Korea, the traditional buildings of palaces and temples are painted with amazingly bright colored geometrical patterns.

The Sutra Hall(Kumsan-sa temple)

Built on the slopes of striking Mt. Chiri-san, Hwaom-sa Temple is one of Korea's most beautiful places.

other treasures. Among them, the five-storey pagoda is thought to date from the Koryo period. It is Treasure No. 25 and is rather different from other pagodas of the period. Possibly this difference is the result of some foreign influence. Next to the five-storey pagoda is a stone bell, a pagoda shaped like a bell, Treasure No. 26, similar to the one at T'ongdo-sa and the one which holds Master Naong's ashes at Shilluk-sa. It probably dates from early Koryo and the technique used in carving it is very refined. This form of pagoda is thought to have been imported from India. There are Buddhas and guardians carved on the face of the stone. The stone lotus support or pedestal is Treasure No. 23 and thought to date from the 10th century. It is to the southeast of the Main Hall and shows a very refined level of carving. The upper lotus is open, the lower lotus is finely balanced with the upper one. There is also a stone lamp, Treasure No. 828; an incense burner stand; a Dew Pillar, Treasure No. 22, of undetermined use; and a flagpole, Treasure No. 28.

The Temple Named after a Philosophy: Hwaom-sa

Hwaom-sa Temple's name is taken directly from that of one of the most influential texts in the history of Korean

Temple Compound (Hwaom-sa temple)

The Main Hall(Kakhwangjon, Hwaom-sa temple, Nat'l Treasure No. 67)

Buddhism: the Avatamsaka Sutra. The underlying theme of the text is the universal oneness of all things.

Built on the slopes of striking Mt. Chiri-san, Hwaom-sa Temple is one of Korea's most beautiful places. Records state that the site was between the kingdoms of Shilla and Paekje and that it was first selected by Master Yon-gi in 554 in the reign of King Chinhung (r. 540-576). Master Uisang expanded the temple in 634 when he introduced the Avatamsa philosophy. The temple was destroyed by the Hideyoshi Invasion and rebuilt by Master Pyogam in 1630 under King Injo (r. 1623-1649).

The temple follows the one Main Hall-twin pagoda pattern on a north-south axis of the Unified Shilla Period. In this plan, two pagodas were built in front of one Main Hall in the main courtyard. In Hwaom-sa, the eastern pagoda, Treasure No. 132, is an unadorned five-storey

*Three-storied Lion pagoda
(Hwaom-sa temple,
Nat'l Treasure No. 35)*

pagoda and the western, Treasure No. 133 is a richly decorated double-pedestaled pagoda which is ornamented with the eight divine generals, four guardians and the zodiac animals. The pagodas are respectively Treasures 132 and 133. The Main Hall was built in 1630 and is an important example of middle Choson period architecture; it is Treasure No. 299. The central statue is of Vairocana, the Cosmic Buddha on the right of which is Sakyamuni and on the left is Rochana.

Let us take a look at Rochana Buddha. In Buddhism, depending on the period and the " fashion" (sometimes one Buddha or Bodhisattva is more popular than another), Rochana can be a form of Amitabha, the Nirmanakaya or the mind-made, emanation body. In a triad with Vairocana, the Dharmakaya, or uncontaminated body, Rochana Buddha is the Sambhogakaya or physical form, the enjoyment body, of the Buddha. Then Sakyamuni is the Nirmanakaya or emanation body. There seem to be no hard and fast rules to these identification and they changed constantly.

To the east of the Main Hall is the Judgement Hall in which graphic paintings of the hells can be seen. To the west is the hall dedicated to Avalokitesvara, the Bodhisattva of Compassion. The beautiful coffered ceiling shows a traditional lotus flower decor.

Behind the Main Hall, there is a path which, after about 150 meters, leads to Sambul-am, Hermitage of the Three Buddhas. There in the Thousand Buddhas Hall are statues of Sakyamuni, Amitabha and the Medicine Buddha with

To the left of the
Main Hall is the
Hall of the
Enlightened
Emperor. (Emperor
is a name for the
Buddha, the
Awakened One who
is lord over
himself..)

Bodhisattvas with cap-like diadems. There are shrines of the Big Dipper and the Mountain God as well.

To the left of the Main Hall is the Hall of the Enlightened Emperor. (Emperor is a name for the Buddha, the Awakened One who is lord over himself..) Built in 1702 or 1703, the 160 meters high, double-roofed building is one of the most magnificent in Korea. It is National Treasure No. 67. The large high roof is a tribute to the high rank of the Buddha (who came from a royal caste). Dating from the last century, the ceiling is covered with carved and painted lotuses in mandala form and fine cosmic patterns. The statues on the pedestal are, from the left, Avalokitesvara, Amitabha, Samantabhadra, the Bodhisattva of Practice, Sakyamuni, Manjusri, the Bodhisattva of Wisdom, Prabhutaratna, Gnanakara. This rich and rare configuration combines traits of the Avatamsa School and the Zen School with popular devotional Buddhism.

Originally the building was called Changyukjon. Legend tells that 100 monks prayed for 100 days to build

Interior of the Main Hall(Hwaom-sa temple)

the hall. One night, an old monk dreamt that Manjusri told him how to collect enough money. Each monk must wet his palm and then touch flour. The one to whom the flour didn't stick was the right person; this was Master Songnung. Manjusri instructed him to ask help from the first person he met the next day. This person turned out to be a beggar woman who, after vowing to be reborn in a rich family, died.

A few years later, Master Songnung met a princess who was very pleased to see him. One of her hands had never opened and the master managed to open it. On the palm was written Changyukjon. On seeing this, King Sukchong (r. 1674-1720) decided to help. When the hall was renamed, the king called it Kakhwangjon. Originally the entire Avatamsaka Sutra was carved on granite plates on the walls, but most of it was destroyed by the 16th century invaders. Remaining fragments have been deposited below the statues.

In front of this hall there are two important monuments. One is the six-meter high stone lantern, National Treasure No. 12. It is the biggest lantern in Korea. The other is a lion pagoda which is Treasure No. 300. Four sitting lions support a pagoda and each lion's face seems to express a different emotion. Both of these stone objects date from 670.

Behind the hall, up a steep path, there is another lion pagoda. It also dates from the 7th century and is National Treasure No. 35. Four crouching lions on a relief-adorned pagoda carry an elegant granite reliquary, the roof of which is layered downward in typical Shilla style. Between the lions is the figure of a nun standing facing a stone lantern a few meters away. She is the mother of the temple founder Yon-gi, who himself is said to be crouching under the stone lantern opposite offering a cup of tea.

Hwaom-sa Temple, set in beautiful mountainous countryside, is a wonderful place to go.

Temple of the Life of the Buddha Hall: Popju-sa

Two kilometers before the entrance to the temple is a tree many might miss. It is a 600 year-old pine tree near the road. Legend tells that it bowed its branches in front of King Sejo ? a story of guilt. King Sejo was the second son of King Sejong; he succeeded the throne by murdering his nephew. In old age he suffered from a severe skin ailment and tried to find solace from his ailment as well as his bad conscience in the forests of Sogni-san Mountain.

One day he met a young woman whose two boys called him grandfather. The woman was Princess Uisook, Sejo's daughter, who had to flee her father because she had pleaded for the life of the murdered nephew. At this meeting the king begged for forgiveness and invited these members of his family back to the palace. The princess refused saying that she preferred her simple life and she later fled further south.

Located on Songni-san Mountain, Popju-sa, "The Dharma Staying" temple, is believed to have been founded in 553, during the reign of King Chinhung; Master Uisang helped build it up. There is a record which states that, at times, 3,000 monks lived here. Eight times renovated, the last occasion was in 1906. Popju-sa is a Head Temple and has some 27 lesser temples under it.

A View of the Temple Compound (Popju-sa temple)

Wooden Pagoda containing pictures of the Life of the Buddha (Palsang-jon, Popju-sa temple, Nat'l Treasure No. 55)

Behind the entrance gate there are two granite pillars dating from 11th century which were used to support the temple painting for special occasions.

In a pavilion on the right side is the 2.70-meter diameter iron pot dating from 720. There is a record which states that the pot was used in the 12th century to serve monks and pilgrims.

The Main Hall or Hall of Great Light is a shrine to Vairocana, Sakyamuni and Rochana. Behind these three images there are three paintings of the Buddhas accompanied by enlightened disciples, Bodhisattvas as well as by a youthful Ananda and a very elderly Kasyapa. Sakyamuni and Rochana are surrounded by rainbows and Vairocana is surrounded by a huge white halo, symbolizing the absolute.

The five-storey pagoda, the oldest wooden pagoda in Korea, was originally built in 553; it is National Treasure No. 55.

The five-storey pagoda, the oldest wooden pagoda in Korea, was originally built in 553; it is National Treasure No. 55. A copy of this pagoda was made in Nara 50 years later at Horiuji. (In Japan, the original pagodas are still standing but in Korea they've all been destroyed by the numerous invasions. A copy of the original pagoda is in the Seoul National Museum.) This one was constructed in 1624 and it has been carefully preserved since then. It is a "Life of the Buddha" or "Eight Paintings Hall" with large murals telling the story of the life of Sakyamuni Buddha; the paintings are not in chronological order. The beautifully carved beams are painted in special designs. Around the central pillar, Buddhists circumambulate as a practice of remembering the Buddha and the task before them to

In front of the
paintings, there
are 340 little white
Buddhas
representing the
innumerable
beings in all places
in all world
systems.

understand his teachings. There are four statues of Sakyamuni, each one facing one of the four cardinal directions, each one showing a different mudra or hand position. The Buddha facing east has the pose of fearlessness, the one facing west is in the pose of Turning the Wheel of the Dharma (teaching), the one facing south shows the earth touching pose and the Buddha facing the north is lying down, Buddha in the dying pose — very rare in Korea. The entourage shows Bodhisattvas and disciples brightly clad and bejewelled. There are some women among the followers.

In front of the paintings, there are 340 little white Buddhas representing the innumerable beings in all places in all world systems. These images are often called disciples even though they actually have the marks of Buddhas. These marks include the long ears, the curled hair and the bump on the head.

Gazing down at the pagoda is a 33-meter high, 160 ton copper Maitreya Buddha. In 1872, King Kojong's father took the Maitreya Buddha statue made by Chinp'yo. In 1939, a new statue was started but couldn't be completed. So in 1964, President Park donated money for a new statue and this allowed the temple to finish the statue

*Enlight Disciples in front of
the paintings in the pagoda
(Popju-sa temple)*

*Interior of the Palsang-jon
(Popju-sa temple)*

The temple has had many famous masters living and teaching in it. Kyongho (1849-1912), a well-known, present-day master lived here.

with cement. In 1990, the statue was replaced with this bronze one.

Nearby there is a two-meter high statue of a woman carrying a pot in her hands. The statue is reputed to be Sujata who offered food to the Buddha just before he attained enlightenment.

Other treasures include a four-meter stone lantern which is Treasure No. 15. There's also a water basin, National Treasure No. 64, shaped like a half-opened magnolia flower. It used to stand in front of the previous Maitreya Hall and is a symbol of the pond in the paradise of the Future Buddha. The lion lantern, National Treasure No. 5, consists of a rare Shilla lantern about 3.3-meters in height dating from 720, made during the reign of King Sondok (r. 702-737).

Tourists may enjoy the many trails leading up to different hermitages and to the peak of Mt. Songni-san.

The Temple of the Ancient Main Hall: Sudok-sa

According to temple records Sudok-sa was founded by Master Sungje in the late Paekje period. It is further recorded that, during the reign of King Uija (r. 641-660), Master Sungje taught the Lotus Sutra in 647 at the temple. There is also another record which states that the temple was founded by one Master Chimyong in 599 during the reign of Paekje King Pop (r. 599-600).

The temple has had many famous masters living and teaching in it. Kyongho (1849-1912), a well-known, present-day master lived here. He ordained quite young and when he was 31, while on

The Main Hall(Sudok-sa temple, Nat'l Treasure No. 49)

his way to Seoul, he saw many dead people from a recent cholera epidemic. This changed his life and he practiced hard and attained true understan-ding. He was the teacher of many great monks, one of the best known was Master Mangong (1872-1946) who also lived at Sudok-sa and where, it is recorded, he gave a special teaching in 1898. Another personality connected with the history of the temple was a nun called Iryop (1869-1971) who lived in Kyongsong-am hermitages. She was a famous writer.

One of the main temples of Korea where there is a comprehensive training center comprised of a meditation hall, a monks' college and a center for studying monks' rules, Sudok-sa also has a Panjang, a Spiritual Master. There are five of these specially selected masters in Korea at any one time. In addition to Sudok-sa, there is one at Haein-sa, one at T'ongdo-sa, one at Songgwang-sa, and one at Paekyang-sa. The Chogye Order has a Secular Leader who is elected for four years of office and a Spiritual Leader who holds office for ten years. At present (1998) the master of T'ongdo-sa holds that position.

When visiting Sudok-sa, you pass through the dragon-ornamented granite One-pillar Gate in order to reach the main monastery compound. The compound is terraced and one interesting feature of the arrangement of the buildings is the fact that the old meeting hall is out of line of the main axis of the temple buildings. In front of it is a three-storey Shilla pagoda which was erected in the second half of the 7th century.

Inside the main courtyard area, there is a second, older seven-storey granite pagoda dating from the early 7th century, or from the Paekje Kingdom. It has the typical curved-up edges to the roofs on each of its storeys. The nearby lantern is modern, copied from an ancient one.

The Main Hall, National Treasure No. 49, is a shrine to an important triad. It was built in 1308 and is the oldest wooden building in Korea of which there is a definite record of the year of construction. It is nothing short of a miracle that the building has stood through successive invasions in which everything of any value seems to have been destroyed almost everywhere else in the country. Its recorded history and the beauty of the design make it extremely important to Korean culture.

Inside there are three Buddhas and two Bodhisattvas.

Inside the main courtyard area, there is a second, older seven-storey granite pagoda dating from the early 7th century, or from the Paekje Kingdom.

Three Storied Stone Pagoda
(Sudok-sa Temple)

On the way to Chonghye-sa, a small temple above Sudok-sa, about 15 minutes walk up the mountain there is a ten-meter granite statue of Maitreya, the Future Buddha.

The three Buddhas represent some of the main features of Buddhism. Sakyamuni is the Historical Buddha, the original teacher. Amitabha is the Buddha of Infinite Light and Bhaisagyaguru is the Medicine Buddha, the Universal Healer. In addition there are two Bodhisattvas: Manjusri, Perfect Wisdom, and Samantabhadra, Perfect Practice. There is a legend which tells that the original paintings on the ceiling and pillars were done by a Koguryo master. On the back wall of the hall is a painting of Ksitigarbha and the Ten Judges and to the right there is another painting of the gods who are indigenous to Korea. Unfortunately, the wall paintings, National Treasure No. 48, created during the Koryo Period, have not been so lucky. Most of them were destroyed in the Korean War and the remaining ones have been moved to the museum. These paintings are famous for their elegant, realistic style and they demonstrate the magnificence of Koryo art. In front of the Main Hall there is a beautifully balanced Unified Shilla Period stupa, Provincial Tangible Cultural Asset No. 103. The stupas of that period capture some loveliness which was lost in the succeeding generations of art. The proportions of the storeys, the curve of the corners, the size of the stands for

The Main Hall(Unmun-sa temple)

Originally called Taejakgap-sa "Great Magpie Hillside" Temple, in 937 the king who founded the Koryo Dynasty changed the name to Unmun-sa, meaning "Cloud Gate" Temple.

each successive layer, all go to make a work of art which cannot fail to please the eye.

On the way to Chonghye-sa, a small temple above Sudok-sa, about 15 minutes walk up the mountain there is a ten-meter granite statue of Maitreya, the Future Buddha. It has a double Korean cylindrical hat, a coat reaching down to the ankles and an imposing attitude in the expression carved on its face. The statue was erected by Mangong.

Nearby is the stupa erected by the disciples of Mangong in memory of their master. It is considered unusual because it has a large spherical stone on the top. There is an inscription on the stupa which reads "The whole world is a single flower."

Unmun-sa Temple

Unmun-sa Temple is one of Korea's major temples and it is situated on Tiger mountain. A Shilla monk built a hermitage on this mountain and, after three years of intensive meditation, he attained enlightenment.

Originally called Taejakgap-sa "Great Magpie Hillside" Temple, in 937 the king who founded the Koryo Dynasty changed the name to Unmun-sa, meaning "Cloud Gate" Temple.

The temple has a famous tree. Said to be 500 years old, legend tells that it grew up from a branch planted by a passing monk.

In 1950, Unmun-sa Temple became the largest bhikkuni training center in Korea. About 250 students regularly follow a three to four year course in Buddhism.

Soknam-sa

"Southern Rock Temple" was built by Toui-kuksa in the 9th century. One of the great monks in the history of Korean Buddhism, Master Toui chose this beautiful spot on Mt. Kaji-san.

At first the temple was small but then it was taken over by bhikkunis in the early part of this century and greatly enlarged. In-hong Sunim was mainly responsible for the development and the creation of three separate meditation halls — one for beginners and experienced practitioners, one for more advanced practitioners and one for three year retreats.

Today the temple has up to 100 ordained women in the meditation season living and practicing together. Ordained women of all ages live here and the traditional style of practice and lifestyle are rigorously followed.

There are two very fine pagodas to visit at this temple as well as enjoying the lovely mountain stream.

One of the great monks in the history of Korean Buddhism, Master Toui chose this beautiful spot on Mt. Kaji-san.

Temples in Seoul

Chogye-sa Temple is the only major temple within the old city walls of Seoul. the temple became the headquarters of Korean Buddhism's Chogye Order.

As many visitors to Korea have little time to visit the temples in the mountains, we thought that it would be good to offer a short description and directions to some of the more famous Seoul temples. Please do take the time to visit some of them, you may be very surprised at the experience!

The Center of the Largest Sect of Korean Buddhism:Chogye-sa

Chogye-sa Temple is the only major temple within the old city walls of Seoul.

Built in 1910, the temple was first called Kakwang-sa. The name was changed to T'aego-sa during the time of the Japanese Occupation and in 1936, the temple became

Interior of the Main Hall (Chogye-sa temple)

This temple hall is a major center of Buddhist events. Nearly every night of the year there is some kind of religious activity going on: a lecture, chanting and bowing classes, special ceremonies and celebrations.

Bathing the Buddha Statue

the headquarters of Korean Buddhism's Chogye Order. It is extremely important to all Korean Buddhists.

In 1954, after the great clean-up movement to rid the country of any vestiges of the Japanese occupation, the temple came to be called Chogye-sa. This is the name of the mountain on which the Sixth Patriarch of Chinese Chan Buddhism, Huineng (638-713), lived. He is highly revered by Korean Buddhists and his life and teachings are constantly studied and remembered.

Born poor and illiterate, Master Huineng attained enlightenment on hearing the Diamond Sutra being chanted while he was selling wood. Eventually he was recognized by the Fifth Patriarch and became his successor. His teachings are simple. One of the most beautiful sayings ascribed to him is a true example of Buddhism. "In all conditions we should be humble and polite." Today, Chogye-sa is the main temple of Korean Buddhism and its major sect, Chogye, which is a Zen sect.

The Main Hall was built in 1 year and 7 months, from March 1937 until October 1938. It is an impressive, wooden structure which is decorated on the outside with paintings of the Buddha's life and teachings, and huge, wooden latticework doors – well worth taking a careful look at. Inside, the comparatively small Buddha statue is of unknown origin. There is a story told, however, that it came from Tokab-sa in Cholla Province. Behind the statue is a traditional painting. The central figure is Sakyamuni, the Historical Buddha, and on either side of him, from the bottom up, are guardians, Bodhisattvas, and, at the top, there are some of the Buddha's disciples. On either side of the glass case containing the Buddha, on the inside, there are cases containing sutras carved on wooden blocks. The central shrine is flanked by paint-ings of hundreds of Buddhas. They are symbolic of the many Buddhas in the universe and the fact that we are all Buddhas without knowing it!

This temple hall is a major center of Buddhist events. Nearly every night of the year there is some kind of religious activity going on: a lecture, chanting and bowing classes, special ceremonies and celebrations.

Behind the Main Hall of Chogye-sa, is the headquarters of the Chogye Order. All kinds of activities also take place there: visiting monks and dignitaries host meetings; there

Praying Buddhist under lanterns

In the Chogye-sa compound, there is also a 500-year-old white pine tree supposed to have been brought from China; it is Natural Monument No. 7. The tall, zelkova tree beside the pagoda is draped with lanterns on the Buddha's Birthday in May of every year.

are exhibitions; and a weekly newspaper is printed.

In front of the Main Hall is a seven-storey pagoda containing a relic of the Buddha which was brought to Korea by a Sri Lankan monk in 1914. People bow as they pass and make offerings of candles and incense in memory of the Buddha. There are traditional stone lanterns on either side of the pagoda.

In front of the Main Hall to the left, there is Bell Pavilion. There hang the drum, the bell, the gong and the fish, instruments used to regulate temple life and call all willing sentient beings to listen to the liberating words of the Buddha which are chanted at every ceremony. First the drum is rhythmically beaten calling the animals. Then the large bell calls those who suffer and live in the realms of torment – in the morning it is struck 33 times for the different heavenly states and 28 times in the morning. And then the cloud-shaped gong calls the beings of the air. The log carved into the shape of a fish calls all that live in the water. At 4 a.m. and at 6 p.m. in winter and 7 p.m. in summer, every day of every year a monk is in charge of sounding these instruments at Chogye-sa – it is a wonderful sight to see.

Beside the Bell Pavilion, there is a newly constructed traditional building. It houses the offices of the temple in the basement, a meeting hall on the ground floor and the offices of training monks and teaching Buddhism on the floor above.

Behind the Main Hall there is a newly constructed hall, called the "Hall of the Virtuous Kings" and it is dedicated to Amitabha, the Buddha of Universal Light. Beside the principle Buddha, there are Ksitigarbha, the helper of those in trouble and Avalokitesvara, the Bodhisattva of Compassion.

In the Chogye-sa compound, there is also a 500-year-old white pine tree supposed to have been brought from China; it is Natural Monument No. 7. The tall, zelkova tree beside the pagoda is draped with lanterns on the Buddha's Birthday in May of every year. At that time the entire courtyard is filled with lanterns and, standing on the platform of the Main Hall, you can gaze down on the sea of shimmering lotuses.

There are many Buddhist shops just outside Chogye-sa where you can buy books, bells, mokt'aks, statues, and other souvenirs and mementoes.

Hwagye-sa

Hwagye-sa, "Flower Stream Temple" is on Samgag-san Mountain. It was built in 1552 by Master Sinwol during the reign of King Chungjong (r. 1506-1544) the 11th king of the Choson Dynasty, destroyed in 1618, during the reign of King Kwanghaegun (r. 1608-1623) and then rebuilt the following year by Master Dowol.

After 240 years, the temple became so dilapidated that two monks, Yongsun and Pamyun had it repaired in 1865. The statues of Bodhisattva Ksitigarbha and the Ten Judges in the Judgment Hall are especially famous. Beautifully carved by Master Nawong in the late Koryo Dynasty, the figures were brought to Hwagye-sa in 1877 by Queen Mother Chodaebe. After that the temple served the royal family.

There are two famous urns on either side of the Main Hall. These were donated by Queen Hongdaebe, wife of King Hunjong (r. 1834-1849).

Hwagye-sa is the home of the Kwan-um International Zen Center which was started by Seung-san Sunim. Foreign monks and lay people live here practicing the traditional way of life of Korean temples.

To get there:

Hwagye-sa is in the northeast of Seoul.

By bus: Take No. 84 (ask the driver "Hwagye-sa?") to the end and walk up the hill (15 min).

By subway: Take the blue line to Suyu and then walk in and up the hill (about 25 min).

The Main Hall(Chin-gwan-sa temple)

Chin-gwan-sa

Chin-gwan-sa was originally built in 1101 CE. Then in 1403, Sooryuk-sa was built on the ruins of the original temple in memory of the nation's founders. Burnt down during the Korean War, it was rebuilt in 1964 by a bhikkhuni, Chin-gwan Sunim. Now it is a women's temple where between ten and twenty bhikkhunis live.

When you enter the main compound, passing under the building used for the thriving children's meeting on Sunday and other events, the Main Hall is directly in front of you. To the left are the living quarters for the nuns. To the right of the Main Hall are smaller shrines. The first hall, recently rebuilt, contains Ksitigarbha with all the judges, the second is the abode of the Mountain God and the Recluse, the third is where people light lamps to remember the departed, and the last is Amitabha's shrine with all the enlightened disciples. The Mountain God's shrine and the one with many small lamps both pre-date the rest of the present temple buildings.

Down to the left there is a path running to the toilets and to the two-storey, new eating hall/kitchen complex. Upstairs there are rooms for senior nuns.

To get there:
By subway: take the orange line in the Kup'abal direction and get down at Yonshinnae. Then get a taxi to the temple.

By bus: take bus no. 154 or 154-1 from in front of the Y.M.C.A. to the end and walk (about 40 min). There are signs at every junction. (There is a small local bus plying back and forth, also.)

Ponguk-sa

Ponguk-sa was built in 1395 by Muhak Desa (1327-1405), a monk who was famous for geomancy and the person who chose the site of Seoul for the capital city of the, then, new Choson Dynasty. At first it was called Yaksa-sa because the main Buddha statue was of the Medicine Buddha or Universal Healer. Muhak Desa hoped that the temple would bring blessings to the new Choson Dynasty so that it would flourish forever. As a result there are all the shrines necessary for bringing good luck in the temple compound. There is a shrine for the Mountain God, one for the Recluse and one for the Seven Stars (the Big Dipper), all traditional shrines of ancient Korea. These are in addition to the more common Hall of Judgment and the Main Hall. There are also living quarters for the monks.

Pongun-sa Temple

The lay-out of the temple is especially pleasing.

To get there: Ponguk-sa is before Pukak Tunnel and Kookmin University.
By bus: Take No. 2 or No. 8 and get down at Ponguk-sa.

Pongun-sa

Pongun-sa was first built during the reign of King Wansong (r. 785-798) by the National Master Yonhoe. In 1551 it became the main temple of the Zen Order. Then, after 1945, it came under the direct control of the Headquarters of the Chogye Order. The main concern of the temple is in education. To this end, there are many programs organized in order to accommodate anyone and everyone. There are different activities for each age group of children and university students, there are discussion and study groups; the temple supports the main Monastic University.

The temple compound is an example of a traditional temple. There are the gates, shrines, and living quarters. A visit to this temple gives the impression of a mountain temple.

To get there: The temple is located on the northern side of KOEX building in the south of Seoul.
By subway: Take green line to Samsong-dong walk north.

Pulgwang-sa

Pulgwang-sa, "Buddha's Light" Temple, is one of Korea's most fascinating temples. The buildings themselves are not so special, it is the orientation of the work being done which is particular. Opened on October 16, 1975, the temple is totally dedicated to social work and aims at helping all members of society. A major activity is the creation of small groups in which anyone can have the opportunity to study the Buddha's teachings and awaken to a clear view of reality.

Understanding the many problems facing people, the temple has organized many support groups. There is a special group that helps members through crises and another aimed at compassionate social work among less fortunate people. Then there is a thriving kindergarten, a publishing company, and various educational programs.

To get there: Pulgwang-sa is in the south of Seoul.

By subway: Take the green line to Chamsil and exit at Lotte World. The temple is to the south of Sokch'on Lake.

Pong-won-sa

Pong-won-sa was originally built on the site of today's Yonsei University in 889 by Master Toson (827-898). In 1748 it was moved to its present site by Master Chanjup. King Yongju wrote an inscription and the temple became known as "New Temple." The present buildings were erected in 1911, but the Main Hall was destroyed during the Korean War. The 3,000 Buddhas' Hall is the largest wooden structure in Korea. Pong-won-sa is the home of the T'aego Order, the second largest in Korea. It is especially famous for traditional ceremonies, chanting, religious dancing and art. At present three national treasures live there: Buddhist Art, Ritual Song and Ritual Ornamentation.

To get there: The temple is in the west of Seoul, behind Yonsei University.

By bus: Take a blue 205 and ask for Pongwon-dong. Get down and walk up the hill (15 min.).

Taegak-sa

Taegak-sa, "Great Enlightenment" Temple, was established in 1894 by Baek, Yong-song Sunim, one of the leaders of the independence movement against the

Japanese. He was a monk who became a hero to Buddhists and non-Buddhists alike. When the government-in-exile returned to Korea from Japan after the Japanese Occupation, they were welcomed at Taegak-sa because of the fame of the founder.

The temple is the place chosen for the translation of the Tripitaka Koreana from Chinese into Korean. This project was started by Yong-song Sunim who wanted to make the Buddha's teachings available to everyone. About 50 of the 6,791 volumes have been translated so far.

In 1987, the temple was largely rebuilt and it continues to be an important place to Korean Buddhists.

To get there: Taegak-sa is in central Seoul, about 10 min. walk from Piwon, the Secret Garden. It is about 15 min walk from Chogye-sa.

By subway: Chong-no 3 Ga station, exit on Chong-no 3 Ga.

By bus: Any bus to the Secret Garden or Chong-no 3 Ga.

Toson-sa

Toson-sa was founded by Master Toson (826-912) who, after traveling far and wide, decided that Samgak-san was the best mountain on which to build a temple because he felt that Buddhism would flourish there. This prophesy was to come true over 1000 years after his death for this is where the famous monk, Master Chungdam (1902-1971) lived.

Master Toson was a very learned monk. He had studied astronomy and geography as well as Buddhism. When he came to Samgak-san he recognized its special features and there, using his magical power, he cut a huge boulder in two and carved a Medicine Buddha on the surface. Today, that 20 foot-high stone Buddha is the source of much wonder and reverence. Many go to visit it and there are stories of people being cured of serious ailments because they had the faith to do their religious practice in this place.

Up, up you go to the temple, perched in the crags on the very top of Samgak-san.

To get there: Tosan-sa is in Ui-dong, in the northeast of Seoul.

By subway: Ui-dong stop and take a No. 6 or 8 bus to the bottom of the hill.

By bus: Take No. 6 or 8 to the end and then walk a little way up. There you will find a bus or jeep provided by the temple or you can walk(about 40 min.).

CHANTS & TEACHINGS

CHANTS & TEACHINGS

Chants

Chanting takes place at every Buddhist ceremony in almost every Buddhist group all over the world. The aim of chanting is to remind ourselves of the Buddha's teachings and share them with others. The main problem with human life is that we forget the lessons we have learned, we forget that desire gets us nowhere, we forget that we are going to die. In addition, the vibrations emanating from the sounds of the voices are considered beneficial to the body and soothing to the mind. In Korea, chanting is usually accompanied by the mokt'ak, a wooden percussion instrument, and, sometimes, a hand bell.

The thrice daily, temple chanting always includes the following two chants: the Heart Sutra and Homage to the Buddhas. The Heart Sutra is one of the most important teachings in Mahayana Buddhism in general, and in Korean Buddhism in particular. Although difficult to understand for those unfamiliar with Buddhism, the reader can catch a glimpse of the transcendental through its lines.

Buddha(Shilla, Nat'l Treasure No. 79)

Heart Sutra

Homage to the Perfection of Wisdom, the lovely, the Holy! Avalokita Bodhisattva was moving in the deep course of the wisdom which has gone beyond. He looked down from on high and saw but five skandhas* which, in their own being, were empty.

"Here, O Sariputra, Form is Emptiness, Emptiness is Form; Form does not differ from Emptiness, Emptiness does not differ from Form; whatever is Empty, that is Form, whatever is Form that is Empty.

The same is true of feelings, perceptions, impulses and consciousness.

O Sariputra, all dharmas are marked with Emptiness, they have no beginning and no end, they are neither imperfect nor perfect, neither deficient nor complete.

Therefore, O Sariputra, in emptiness there is no form, no feeling, no perception, no name, no concepts, no knowledge. No eye,

no ear, no nose, no tongue, no body, no mind; no forms, sounds, smells, tastes, touchables or object of the mind, no sight organ, no hearing organ no smelling organ, no tasting organ, no feeling organ and no mind consciousness element; no ignorance or extinction of ignorance, no decay and death, no extinction of decay and death. There is no suffering, no origination, no stopping, no path, no cognition, no attainment, nor anything to attain.

There is nothing to accomplish and so Bodhisattvas can rely on the Perfection of Wisdom without trouble. Being without trouble, they are not afraid, having overcome anything upsetting, they attain Nirvana.

All Buddhas who appear in the three periods, fully Awake to the utmost, right and perfect enlightenment because they have relied on the Perfection of Wisdom.

Therefore, one should know the Perfection of Wisdom is the great mantra, is the unequaled mantra, the destroyer of suffering. Because of this Truth, listen to the mantra:

Gate, Gate, Paragate, Para Samgate Bodhisvaha
Gate, Gate, Paragate, Para Samgate Bodhisvaha
Gate, Gate, Paragate, Para Samgate Bodhisvaha
Gone, Gone, Gone beyond, Gone utterly beyond
Gone, Gone, Gone beyond, Gone utterly beyond
Gone, Gone, Gone beyond, Gone utterly beyond
Oh what an Awakening!

(*The five skandhas are the five components of any individual: body, perceptions, feelings, mental formations and consciousness.)

Homage to the Buddhas

May the sweet scent of our keeping the precepts, of our meditations, of our wisdom, of our liberation and of the knowledge of our liberation — may all this form a shining cloud-like pavilion and pervade the whole universe. May it do homage to all the countless Buddhas, Dharma and Sanghas in all the ten directions.

*Amitabha Buddha
(Shilla, Nat'l Treasure No. 82)*

Mantra of Incense Offering:
Om-ba-a-ra-to-bi-ya-hum. (3 times)

We most devoutly pay homage to the teacher of all the three worlds, the great teacher of all beings, to our guide, Sakyamuni Buddha.

We devoutly pay homage to the eternally existent assembly of all the Buddhas, in all the ten directions, of the past, present and future as countless as the lands and seas in Lord Indra's net.

We devoutly pay homage to all the Teachings, eternally existent, in all the ten directions, in the past, present, and future as countless as the lands and seas in Lord Indra's net.

We devoutly pay homage to all Bodhisattvas and Mahasattvas, and most especially do we commemorate the Bodhisattvas Manjusri, Sariputra, Samantabhadra, the most compassionate and loving Avalokitesvara, and he, the Lord of many vows, Ksitigarbha.

We devoutly pay homage to the countless compassionate and love-filled Communities, and most especially do we commemorate those who have received personally the Buddha's teachings on Mount Gridhakuta - the ten major disciples, the sixteen holy ones, the five hundred holy ones, and all of the one thousand five hundred great Attained Ones.

We devoutly pay homage to those great patriarchs and teachers who have come from the West to the East, those who have come to Korean shores, and who have transmitted the Light of the Teaching down through all generations. Likewise we pay homage to masters of all traditions, recognized throughout the ages, and to our various numberless spiritual teachers and friends.

We devoutly pay homage to all Sanghas, eternally existent, in all the ten directions, of the past, present, and future as countless as the lands and seas in Lord Indra's net.

We earnestly desire that the inexhaustible Three Precious Ones will most lovingly and compassionately receive our devotions, and that they will empower us spiritually; we further most earnestly desire that together with all creatures in the universe, we may attain Buddhahood at one and the same time.

Teachings

The Precepts

A Buddhist is a person who takes refuge in the Buddha, the Teachings and the Community of Buddhists and who takes five training rules, precepts, by which he lives his life. Although the same in all schools of Buddhism, in Korea they are expressed as follows:

The First Precept: I take the training rule of abstaining from killing and henceforth practice loving-kindness.

Killing roots out the seeds of love and compassion. To kill another is to feast on our friends and relatives from previous lives. It leads to rebirth in painful states and does not give us rebirth in the human body necessary for attaining enlightenment.

The Second Precept: I take the training rule of not taking things which have not been given and of practicing generosity.

Takings things which have not been given to us roots out virtue and wisdom. By desiring things belonging to someone else, we allow greed to grow and we behave like animals.

The Third Precept: I take the training rule

Maitreya Bodhisattva
(Shilla, Nat'l Treasure No. 81)

of controlling sensual and sexual desire and of practicing awareness.

Lack of control of the senses destroys the seeds of purity and simplicity. It leads to a life of no peace and stability and a future in the lower realms.

The Fourth Precept: I take the training rule of not lying, gossiping or speaking harshly and of practicing wholesome speech.

The tongue is sharper than the sword, wrong speech destroys the seeds of truth and cuts off the flowers of goodwill. The only future for one who is careless of speech is suffering.

The Fifth Precept: I take the training rule of refraining from intoxicants which cloud the mind and of practicing clear mindedness.

Alcohol and drugs destroy wisdom and cause behavior which creates piles of regrets. Practice awareness and live a life free from regret!

Ten Guides Along the Path ("Powang Sammaeron")

Here is a popular and much loved text. It's common sense and clear message inspire and encourage all those who study it.

1. Why hope for perfect health? Perfect health leads only to greater greed. "Treat illness as medicine, not disease."

2. Why long for a life free from hardship? Such a life leads only to haughtiness and self-pampering. "Make worries and hardships a way of life."

3. Why hope for a lack of impediments in your study? "Release is hiding right behind obstructions."

4. Why hope for a lack of temptations in your training? A lack of temptations will only serve to soften your resolve. "Treat temptations as friends who are helping you along the way."

5. Why hope for easy success? Easy accomplishment leads only to increased rashness. "Accomplish through difficulties."

6. Why hope to get your way with friends? Having friends give in to your wishes only leads to arrogance. "Make long-term friends through compromise in your relationships."

7. Why expect people to follow your wishes or commands? This, too, leads to arrogance. "Consider those who differ with you to be your character builders."

8. Why expect rewards for your kindnesses? This leads only to a scheming mind. "Throw out the expectation of rewards like you'd throw out old shoes."

9. Why expect more out of life than you deserve? Exaggerated profit-seeking leads only to foolishness. "Become rich at heart with small amounts."

10. Why complain about vexations? This leads only to resentment and poison in the heart. "Consider vexations as the first door on the path."

Greedless Harmony

A talk given by a modern Korean master,
Ven. Songch'ol
(1912-1993)

The sons and daughters of Buddha are free on the eternal path of liberation, and the sons and daughters of Confucius sing of the Great Age of Sages. The sons and daughters of Jesus are replete in their infinite glory, and the sons and daughters of Mohammed have hearts bursting with joy and happiness.

The world is a single home, and all of mankind is one. So let's forget such useless discrimination as "self" and "others," and forget national, racial and other barriers.

Medicine Buddha(Shilla)

Let's treat those of other religions as members of our own, and those of other nations as our compatriots.

To harm others is to harm yourself, and to help others is to help yourself. Treat the sick as if they were yourself, and serve the anguished in every way that you can.

It is awful to disguise personal profit and greed as patriotism and fraternity, so let's rid ourselves of this completely. With a pure heart, let's all help one another and let's all trust one another. Let's respect one another and love one another, and let's all harmonize as one.

As I sit leisurely without thoughts of "self" and "others," plum blossoms begin to cast their fragrance into falling snow.

Sarira Reliquary, Gilt Bronze and Crystal(Shilla, Treasure No. 366)

Inspiring Yourself to Practice

(English translation by Won-myong Sunim and Mark Mueller)

Introduction

Inspiring Yourself to Practice *was written by the Shilla Monk Wonhyo (617-686). It consists of 706 characters, contained in one roll. In Korea, the text is one of the most important in the curriculum of the temple training, during the period of study. The text stresses the need to eliminate one's karmic bond with the world and to begin immediately to practice. The original Chinese text is kept at Haein-sa Temple, near Taegu, and the annotated version is kept at Songgwang-sa Temple, in Sunchon.*

* Numbers in the text refer to explanatory notes at the end.

All the Buddhas
Who reside within the splendid realm of Nirvana
Have, throughout countless eons,
Discarded their desires and undergone arduous training.

Sentient beings
That transmigrate within the burning house of desire
Have, for countless generations,
Failed to discard their greed and desire.

The gates to heaven (the Pure Land)
Are not blocked;
Yet, few are those who enter them.

This is because most people make their home
Among the three poisons.[1]

The evil realms[2] have no real power to seduce us,
Yet many enter them.
The deluded mind values
The four elements[3] that make up the body

And the five desires[4]
As if they were jewels.

This being so,
Is there anyone who does not long
To retire to the seclusion of the mountains
In order to practice the Way?[5]

Yet people do not go there;
They remain caught up in desire.

Medicine Buddha
(Shilla, Treasure No. 328)

Although you do not
Retire to the mountains
To cultivate your mind,
You should strive with all your energy
To perform good deeds.

If you can renounce your own pleasure,

You will become as trusted and respected
As the sages.
If you can undergo
That which is difficult,
You will become as respected
As the Buddha.

Those who greedily seek after things
Join the ranks of demons.

Those who give with compassion
Are the disciples of the Dharma King.

High mountains and lofty peaks
Are where the wise reside.
Green pines and deep mountain valleys
Are home to those who practice.
When hungry, such people pick fruit from trees
To calm their empty stomach.
When thirsty, they quench their thirst
With water from a stream.

Although we eat fine foods
In an attempt to carefully preserve this body,
Our bodies will definitely face destruction;
Even though we cover this body
With soft cloth,
Our lives are sure to come to an end.

1) Greed, hatred (anger) and stupidity (ignorance).
2) Durgati, the hell realm, the animal realm, etc.; there are 3, 4, or 5 according to text consulted.
3) Earth, water, fire and air are the four elements that everything is made of.
4) There are two meanings:
   1] the objects of the 5 senses (eye, ear, nose, mouth, body); these defile the True Nature when the mind is filled with desire;
   2] desire for wealth, sex, food, fame, and sleep.
5) The Way refers to the path to enlightenment.

Make a small mountain cave where echoes resound
Into a hall to chant the Buddha's name.
Let the sad cry of a wild goose
Be the heart-warming call of a friend.

While bowing, your knees may become
As cold as ice,
But you must not long for a warm fire.
Your stomach may writhe with hunger,
But you must not give in to your thoughts of food.

One hundred years pass like the blinking of an eye,
So why don't you practice?
How long is a lifetime?
Can you afford to neglect practice,
Wasting your time on leisure?

It is only he who renounces
All of the desires in his heart
That is rightfully called a practicing monk.
Only he who no longer yearns for the ways of the world

Is called "a monk who has renounced the house-holder's life."[6]

A practitioner who is caught
Within the net of worldly desires
Is like a dog who wears
Elephant's hide.
A man who practices the Way
Yet remains attached to worldly desire
Is like a hedgehog
Who tries to enter a rat hole.

Some people, in spite of their outstanding ability and wisdom,
Choose to live in the busy atmosphere of the city.

All the Buddhas feel pity and concern for such people.

Other people, although they have not yet developed
A deep practice,
Still choose to stay in the contemplative atmosphere of the mountains.
The sages feel a great joy
When they see such people.[7]

There are those who are skilled and learned,
But do not follow the precepts.
They are like men who are told of a cache of jewels
But do not get up and go to it.

There are those who practice steadfastly
But lack wisdom.
They are like men who want to go east
But mistakenly walk towards the west.
The actions of a wise man
Are like steaming grains of rice
In order to make a bowl of rice.
The actions of a man who lacks wisdom
Are like steaming grains of sand
In order to make a bowl of rice.
Everyone knows how to eat and drink
In order to satiate their hunger;
But no one seems to understand
The method of training –

6) When a person is ordained in Buddhism, he is said to have gone forth from household life. The idea is that leaving all the problems of family and home behind, he can better dedicate him/herself to spiritual attainment.
7) This is because city dwellers have little possibility of spiritual development but those living in the country, though they may not be advanced, have a good chance.

The way to transform the ignorant mind.

Practice and wisdom must exist side by side.
For they are like the two wheels of a cart.
Likewise, helping oneself and helping others
Are like the two wings of a bird.

If you absent-mindedly chant for your donors
Over the morning offering of porridge
Without understanding the meaning,
You should feel ashamed
To face those who give alms.

If you chant
During the lunch-time ceremony
Without attaining the essence of the words you utter,
Won't you be ashamed to face
Great people and sages?

Everyone hates squirming insects
And those who can't distinguish between the dirty and the clean.
Likewise, the sages feel disgust with those monks
Who cannot distinguish between the defiled and the pure.
If you wish to be through with this world's conflict,
Good conduct is the ladder
That ascends to heaven.

Therefore, one who violates the precepts
And yet wishes to help others
Is like a bird with broken wings
That puts a turtle on its back and tries to fly.

If you're still not free from your own faults,
You will not be able to free others of their faults.
So why do you, who violate the precepts
Receive that which is provided by others?

It does not benefit you in the least
To merely maintain your physical body

If you neglect to practice.
And all your concern for this transient, fleeting life
Will not preserve it.

If you've set your sights
On the virtue of the great masters,
You must endure even the longest hardships.
Once you've set out for the Tiger Throne,[8]
You must forever leave all your desires behind you.

When the cultivator's mind is pure,
All the devas[9] bow in praise of him.
When a follower of the Way loves lasciviousness,
The good spirits leave him.

At death, when the four elements of the body scatter,
You cannot preserve the body and remain in it any longer.
Today, evening has already arrived;
Tomorrow morning will soon be here.

8) This is a name for the Dharma Seat, the special platform that a great monk sits on to give a Dharma lecture. Someone aiming to sit on this seat is aiming for enlightenment and so has to give up all attachments and desires.
9) The devas are the gods, beings who live in realms of constant pleasure.

So, practice now before it is too late.

Worldly pleasures are unsatisfactory;
Why do you greedily cling to them?
Enduring joy can be won through a single
effort in patience;
Why won't you practice?

Those who practice feel shame
To see a seeker of the Way who remains
attached to greed.
The virtuous man
laughs
At the seeker who
forsakes the householder's
life
But is still wealthy.

Words, such as these
written here, go on and on,

Yet clinging attachment does not
come to an end.
"I'll do it next time" -
such words go on and on,
Yet you fail to put an
end to clinging.
Clinging goes on and on,
Yet you fail to renounce worldly
matters.
Your mind is filled with endless
devious plans,
Yet you do not make up your mind to put
an end to them.
"Today will be different," you say,
Yet you continue to perform evil actions
every day.
"Tomorrow, tomorrow," you say,
Yet few are the days when you really do
something good.
"This year will be different," you say,
Yet your defilements are without end.
"Next year I'll do it," you say,

*Incense Burner,
Bronze Inlaid
with Silver*

Yet you don't grow in wisdom.

The hours pass,
And too soon a day and night are over.
The days pass,
And soon it's the last day of the month.
The months pass,
And suddenly another new year has
come.
The years pass,
And in the blinking
of an eye,
We find ourselves
at death's door.

A broken cart
Cannot be driven.
When you're an old man,
You cannot begin to
practice.
When you lie down,
You will succumb to laziness.
And when you sit,

Your mind will be
overwhelmed
With stray thoughts.

For many lifetimes, you have
failed to practice,
Passing your days and nights in
vain.
Having lived many lifetimes in vain,
Will you again fail to practice during this
lifetime?

This body will inevitably come to an end;
Who knows what body you will have next
time?

Isn't this an urgent matter?
Isn't this an urgent matter?

Appendix I: Glossary

BCE, Before Common Era, and CE, Common Era, are the now accepted replacements for the traditional BC and AD respectively.

Buddha relic (A relic is known as "sari" in Korean and it is the calcified remains of a body after cremation. They are held to be an indication of spiritual attainment and highly valued and venerated all over the Buddhist world. A Buddha relic is considered to be a relic of the Historical Buddha, Sakyamuni.).

Buddha triad is a group of Buddhas or a Buddha and Bodhisattvas. The personalities chosen to be put together vary according to the period of history and the wishes of the donor. Though mostly large statues placed in temples, it was the custom to make triads in a smaller portable form, a kind of traveling shrine.

Buddhist texts consist of three parts. These are the Vinaya, the sutras and the Abhidharma. The Vinaya is the collection of rules which were created when problems or special situations arose with the group of people living with the Buddha. The sutras are the teachings, mostly given by the Buddha, in answer to questions or as direction to the community. The Abhidharma is the Higher Philosophy, a systematized consideration of mind and mental processes.

A mokt' ak is a wooden "bell" which is struck in order to keep the chanting together or for calling the members of the community together.

Samguk-yusa, (Memorabilia of the Three Kingdoms) written by Master Iryon in the 13th century is a kind of history book containing many ancient Korean legends.

Appendix II: Dynastic Lineages

(Wang, Kosogan, Isagum, Maripkan are all words for "King"; Yowang for "Queen")

Koguryo (37 BCE - 668 CE)

1. Tongmyong Wang
   (37 BCE-19 BCE)

2. Yuri(myong) Wang
   (19 BCE-18 CE)

3. Taemusin Wang
   (r. 18-44)

4. Minjung Wang
   (r. 44-48)

5. Mobon Wang
   (r. 48-53)

6. T'aejo Wang
   (r. 53-146)

7. Ch'adae Wang
   (r. 146-165)

8. Shindae Wang
   (r. 165-179)

9. Kogukch'on Wang
   (r. 179-196)

10. Sansang Wang
    (r. 196-227)

11. Tongch'on Wang
    (r. 227-248)

12. Chungch'on Wang
    (r. 248-270)

13. Soch'on Wang
    (r. 270-292)

14. Pongsang Wang
    (r. 292-300)

15. Mich'on Wang
    (r. 300-331)

16. Kogugyang Wang
    (r. 331-371)

17. Sosurim Wang
    (r. 371-384)

18. Koguguyang Wang
    (r. 384-391)

19. Kwanggaet'o Wang
    (r. 391-413)

20. Changsu Wang
    (r. 413-491)

21. Munja(myong) Wang
    (r. 491-519)

22. Anjang Wang
    (r. 519-531)

23. Anwon Wang
    (r. 531-545)

24. Yangwon Wang
    (r. 545-559)

25. P'yongwon Wang
    (r. 559-590)

26. Yongyang Wang
    (r. 590-618)

27. Yongnyu Wang
    (r. 618-642)

28. Pojang Wang
    (r. 642-668)

Paekje (18 BCE - 660 CE)

1. Onjo Wang
   (18 BCE-28 C.E)

2. Taru Wang
   (r. 28-77)

3. Kiru Wang
   (r. 77-128)

4. Kaeru Wang
   (r. 128-166)

5. Ch"ogo Wang
   (r. 166-214)

6. Kusu Wang
   (r. 214-234)

7. Saban Wang
   (r. 234)

8. Koi Wang
   (r. 234-286)

9. Ch"aekkye Wang
   (r. 286-298)

10. Punso Wang
    (r. 298-304)

11. Piryu Wang
    (r.304-344)

12. Kye Wang
    (r.344-346)

13. Kun Ch"ogo Wang
    (r. 346-375)

14. Kun Kusu Wamg
    (r. 375-384)

15. Ch'imnyu Wang
    (r. 384-385)

16. Chinsa Wang
    (r. 385-392)

17. Ashin(Ahwa) Wang
    (r. 392-405)

18. Chonji Wang
    (r. 405-420)

19. Kuishin Wang
    (r. 420-427)

20. Piyu Wang
    (r. 427-455)

21. Kaero Wang
    (r. 455-475)

22. Munju Wang
    (r. 475-477)

23. Samgun Wang
    (r. 477-479)

24. Tongsong Wang
    (r. 479-501)

25. Muryong Wang
    (r. 501-523)

26. Song Wang
    (r. 523-554)

27. Widok Wang
    (r. 554-598)

28. Hye Wang
    (r. 598-599)

29. Pop Wang
    (r. 599-600)

30. Mu Wang
    (r. 600-641)

31. Uija Wang
    (r. 641-660)

Shilla (57 BCE - 935 CE)

1. Hyokkose Kosogan
   (57 BCE-4.CE)

2. Namhae Ch'ach'aung
   (r. 4-24)

3. Yuri Isagum
   (24-57)

4. T'arhae Isagum
   (r. 57-80)

5. P'asa Isagum
   (r. 80-112)

6. Chima Isagum
   (r. 112-134)

7. Ilsong Isagum
   (r. 134-154)

8. Adalla Isagum
   (r. 154-184)

9. Porhyu Isagum
   (r. 184-196)

10. Naehae Isagum
    (r. 196-230)

11. Chobun Isagum
(r. 230-247)

12. Ch' omhae Isagum
(r. 247-261)

13. Mich' u Isagum
(r. 262-284)

14. Yurye Isagum
(r. 284-298)

15. Kirim Isagum
(r. 298-310)

16. Hurhae Isagum
(r. 310-356)

17. Naemul Maripkan
(r. 356-402)

18. Shilsong Maripkan
(r. 402-417)

19. Nulchi Maripkan
(r. 417-458)

20. Chabi Maripkan
(r. 458-479)

21. Soji Maripkan
(r. 479-500)

22. Chijung Wang
(r. 500-514)

23. Pophung Wang
(r. 514-540)

24. Chinhung Wang
(r. 540-576)

25. Chinji Wang
(r. 576-579)

26. Chinp' yong Wang
(r. 579-632)

27. Sondok Yowang
(r. 632-647)

28. Chindok Yowang
(r. 647-654)

29. (T'aejong) Muyol Wang
(r. 654-661)

30. Mummu ang
(r. 661-681)

31. Shimmun Wang
(r. 681-692)

32. Hyoso Wang
(r. 692-702)

33. Songdok Wang
(r. 702-737)

34. Hyosong Wang
(r. 737-742)

35. Kyongdok Wang
(r. 742-765)

36. Hyegong Wang
(r. 765-780)

37. Sondok Wang
(r.780-785)

38. Wonsong Wang
(r. 785-798)

39. Sosong Wang
(r. 798-800)

40. Aejang Wang
(r. 800-809)

41. Hondok Wang
(r. 809-826)

42. Hungdok Wang
(r. 826-836)

43. Huigang Wang
(r. 836-838)

44. Minae Wang
(r. 838-839)

45. Sinmu Wang
(r. 839)

46. Munsong Wang
(r. 839-857)

47. Honan Wang
(r. 857-861)

48. Kyongmun Wang
(r. 861-875)

49. Hon-gang Wang
(r. 875-886)

50. Chonggang Wang
(r. 886-887)

51. Chinsong Yowang
(r. 887-897)

52. Hyogong Wang
(r. 897-912)

53. Sindok Wang
(r. 912-917)

54. Kyongmyong Wang
(r. 917-924)

55. Kyongae Wang
(r. 924-927)

56. Kyongsun Wang
(r. 927-935)

Koryo (918 - 1392)

1. T'aejo
(r. 918-943)

2. Hyejong
(r. 943-945)

3. Chongjong
(r. 946-949)

4. Kwangjong
(r. 949-975)

5. Kyongjong
(r. 975-981)

6. Songjong
(r. 981-997)

7. Mokchong
(r. 997-1009)

8. Hyonjong
(r. 1009-1031)

9. Tokchong
(r. 1031-1034)

10. Chongjong
(r. 1035-1046)

11. Munjong
(r. 1046-1083)

12. Sunjong
(r. 1083)

13. Sonjong
(r. 1083-1094)

14. Honjong
(r.1094-1095)

15. Sukchong
(r. 1095-1105)

16. Yejong
(r. 1105-1122)

17. Injong
(r. 1122-1146)

18. Uijong
(r. 1146-1170)

19. Myongjong
(r. 1170-1197)

20. Shinjong
(r. 1197-1204)

21. Huijong
(r. 1204-1211)

22. Kangjong
(r. 1211-1213)

23. Kojong
(r. 1213-1259)

24. Wonjong
(r. 1259-1274)

25. Ch'ungyol Wang
(r. 1274-1308)

26. Ch'ungson Wang
(r. 1308-1313)

27. Ch'ungsuk Wang
(r. 1313-1330)
(r. 1332-1339)

28. Ch'unghye Wang
(r. 1330-1332)
(r. 1339-1344)

29. Ch'ungmok Wang
(r. 1344-1348)

30. Ch'ungjong ang
(r. 1348-1351)

31. Kongming Wang
(r. 1351-1374)

32. U Wang
(r. 1374-1388)

33. Ch' ang Wang
(r. 1388-1389)

34. Kongyang Wang
(r. 1389-1392)

Choson (1392 - 1910)

1. T' aejo
(r. 1392-1398)

2. Chongjong
(r. 1398-1400)

3. T''aejong
(r. 1400-1418)

4. Sejong
(r. 1418-1450)

5. Munjong
(r. 1450-1452)

6. Tanjong
(r. 1452-1455)

7. Sejo
(r. 1455-1468)

8. Yejong
(r. 1468-1469)

9. Songjong
(r. 1469-1494)

10. Yonsan-gun
(r. 1494-1506)

11. Chungjong
(r. 1506-1544)

12. Injong
(r. 1544-1545)

13. Myongjong
(r. 1545-1567)

14. Sonjo
(r. 1567-1608)

15. Kwanghaegun
(r. 1608-1623)

16. Injo
(r. 1623-1649)

17. Hyojong
(r. 1649-1659)

18. Hyonjong
(r. 1659-1674)

19. Sukchong
(r. 1674-1720)

20. Kyongjong
(r. 1720-1724)

21. Yongjo
(r. 1724-1776)

22. Chongjo
(r. 1766-1800)

23. Sunjo
(r. 1800-1834)

24. Honjong
(r. 1834-1849)

25. Ch' oljong
(r. 1849-1863)

26. Kojong
(r. 1864-1907)

27. Sunjong
(r. 1907-1910)

WHAT IS KOREAN
BUDDHISM?

Published by
Korean Buddhist Chogye Order
45, Kyonji-dong, Chongno-gu, Seoul, Korea.
Tel : 822-720-7060 / 7064
Fax : 822-720-7065

Publisher : Ven. Jeong-Dae
Editor-in-chief : Ven. Jung-Nyun
Photo by : National Museum of Korea
        Kyongju National Museum
        Puyo National Museum
        Kim Seong-Cheol
        Hong Eun-Mi

Publication 9. September 2000
Published by Chogye Order Publishing
Printed in Korea

ISBN 89-86821-00-1
U.S $ 20